Walking

Through

The

Ashes

By

Gary Phillip Holdcroft

To Tom & Barb:
I hope you enjoy
the story.

8-6-13

I am the god of Hellfire

And I bring you

Fire…

I bring you to burn

Fire…

I bring you to learn

I'll see you burn

"The Crazy World of
Arthur Brown"
"Fire" 1969

Introduction

This is *not* the story of the Rodeo-Chediski Fire. This is one man's personal experience during the fire. This is about the things that I saw, heard and felt while helping to battle the largest wildfire in the history of the State of Arizona. I do not believe that it is possible to write a definitive story about the fire because it would have to take into account *everyone* that was touched by this disaster. Every person that was evacuated or lost a home, lost a pet or found a new one, everyone who watched the news reports about the fire, or those who were actually on the frontlines, all have an experience to share.

I purposely did not delve *too* deeply into the politics of this fire. I will leave that to the politicians. I did not go into the legal and judicial aspects of the people who started the fire. I will leave that to the law enforcement officials and the judges. I will leave it to the reader to draw their own conclusions about the Forest Service and the environmentalists.

My hat is off to the many people who worked so hard to help save what could be saved and who fought to put this fire out. It was truly a "monster" and the firefighters were the slayers of the beast. I know that every single one you have your *own* story to tell.

I have tried to be as accurate as possible with the timeline in this story, but going without sleep for days, tends to blur one's perception of time. I extend my apologies to those who would read this as a news article. This is not what this story is intended to be.

I should say that, while I am critical of the Forest Services' plan to attack the fire, I have nothing but respect for the men and women who did the actual work. I know that most of you live in the very same communities that you were trying to save. My gripe is with the people who think that homes and neighborhoods and towns are expendable. You know who you are.

There are other books about the Rodeo-Chediski Fire that go into more technical aspects of firefighting and equipment. There are also books and documents that deal with the post-fire recovery efforts more efficiently than I could ever do. My goal is to shed a more personal light on the fire. I know there are details I've forgotten and people I've left out, but I have tried to give the reader a perspective from someone who was there, in the midst of the fire and smoke.

To the many people who gave of their time and effort, and to the volunteer firefighters on this mountain, I say, thank you. May you wear the brand of "renegade" as a badge of honor.

GPH

Chapter 1

The wind is blowing again. It seems as though it's been blowing for months now. I don't mean a breeze. This is wind. A steady, constant wind of thirty-plus miles per hour with gusts even higher. Dust is kicking up across the roadway and grit pelts your face when you step outside. You would think we were living in the valley. I was used to this kind of dusty, windy spring weather when I lived in Tucson, but here in the high country I expected the weather to be different.

As a young boy, my family would vacation on this mountain. I have vivid memories of romping through the woods with my dog, trout fishing on the banks of Big Lake and afternoon thunderstorms that blew in with such regularity that you could practically set your watch by them. But now, any sort of thunderstorm seems to be hard pressed to develop. The ones that do erupt have little moisture and mostly just throw down bolts of lightning, virga hanging off of the cloud base like wispy mares' tails. The smell of rain hangs in the air, but that is as close as we will get to any moisture. It's maddening.

You can tell that the forest needs rain. Badly. The huge Ponderosa pine trees, whose boughs were once thick and full, are now thin and scrawny. The forest floor, which once had wild strawberry, orchids and onion, now sounds like you are walking on a layer of cornflakes. The dead pine needles are several inches thick. Brown piles of straw that layer the base of the trees. I suppose that when moisture was abundant the needles and leaves would break down and form a compost that sustained the woods. Now, it is a choking mass of debris in dire need of removal. A single spark would set this ablaze in no time.

A fire. That would seem to be what the forest needs. Nature's own gardener. Thinning the underbrush and keeping things tidy, healthy, and sending back to the earth in ash, the nutrients needed to fertilize the new growth and keep the old growth going. This is an ancient balance. One that Mother Nature has devised and which has seemed to work quite well through the millennia. That is, until now.

Drought. I remember hearing this word when I was a boy. I knew that it meant that it hadn't rained in awhile. That was about the extent of its meaning. You see, when you live in the desert, rain is, quite simply, rare. When it does rain, it is a momentous occasion. People are glued to the weather reports to hear when the next chance of rain will be. A good thunderstorm is all that is talked about for days, maybe weeks, depending on how long it has been since the last "measurable" rainfall. Measurable? Any rain to me is measurable. If I feel it on my face, it is rain. If it smears my windshield, it is rain. If it leaves only tiny marks in the dust, it is rain. When there is little or no rain for ninety percent of the year, then, by God, rain is rain.

The locals in Tucson will agree with my recollection of the rainy seasons of the past. It seemed as though in the summer months, the showers would begin at right around five o'clock. Period. Now, I'm sure it didn't happen exactly that way, but when you witness a couple of good five o'clock rain storms, you look back and it seems like it always did. The intensity of the storms seemed different then. They were more volatile. You could watch them build up during the hot afternoons. Small, billowy clouds would continue to grow and expand. At one o'clock there may be a cloud that looks like snow-white cotton candy on the horizon. By three o'clock the same cloud will start taking on an ominous gun-metal blue tint.

Gary Phillip Holdcroft

When five o'clock rolls around, it will appear as though night has fallen to the south. Low, guttural rumblings of thunder can be heard in the distance as the storms intensify. Gray sheets of rain fall from the sky and kick up dust storms ahead of it. Then comes the real rain. Huge drops of water that splat against the roof or the windshield or the asphalt, which is so hot the rain nearly steams as it hits. Rivulets of water begin running through the streets. Rivulets soon turn to streams, which turn to rivers, which turn to floods.

Many of the avenues in Tucson were designed to be drainage systems. The roads that run north and south were particularly notorious for flooding. Columbus Avenue and Alvernon Road are two that come to mind. Great torrents of rainwater would roar down these boulevards, trapping motorists and keeping the fire department very busy. The water would spill into arroyos and end up flowing to the farmlands northwest of Tucson. Though rainfall in frequency is rare, when it does occur it can be quite surprising in its intensity. My point is, nature controls the weather and we simply react to it. At times, we receive rainfall in abundance and other times it is very sparse. That's the nature of living in the desert.

When I moved to the White Mountains in northeastern Arizona I was anticipating a change from the climate of the low deserts. Generally, the mountainous areas receive more rain and, more importantly, snow, than the rest of the state. Being a desert rat nearly all of my life meant that I was accustomed to basically two seasons. There is winter, which is really like six months of spring, and then summer, which is six months of hellish, blast furnace heat. Believe it or not, one actually becomes acclimated to the dual season climate. I know that air conditioning and evaporative cooling are what *really* conquered the West, but ones body does adapt to the heat. However, in making the move northward I was looking to find four seasons. Actually, I was looking for autumn and winter, two seasons that had been missing in my life.

As luck would have it, a drought had been slowly creeping over the western United States. When I first moved to the community of Linden, which is a couple of miles west of Show Low (named for the turn of a card), the drought had been in effect for one or two years. There was really no noticeable difference in the weather to me, but the locals on the mountain were adamant that a drought was in place and it was already taking its toll on various crops, livestock and wildlife. Because I'd only lived here for a few seasons, I didn't notice these changes. But there were signs that even a newcomer could see. I remember seeing photographs on the wall of a local saloon and eatery in town of unusually heavy snowfall from years gone by. Now, granted, these were exceptional years, but the snowfall I had witnessed during my winters on the mountain did not carry a fraction of this amount of snow. I drive for a living and the lack of snow and wintry weather made running my route much easier, but I would prefer to have the type of weather for which I had moved to the mountains.

The seasonal wind shift, known as "the monsoon" in Arizona, provides the fuel for the summer storms, but what was sorely lacking for these past few years was snow pack. Snow pack provides a slow, seeping type of moisture feed that replenishes the groundwater table and allows the Ponderosa and spruce trees to draw up the moisture needed to make sap. This sap not only makes the tree more full and healthy, but also provides a natural protection from insects such as the many varieties of bark beetle.

The male bark beetle invades the tree by chewing into the bark and then releasing a pheromone that attracts other beetles to the tree. They proceed to devour the cambium layer of the tree, which lies right under the bark and, as an added attraction, they introduce a parasite known as blue fungus that deprives the tree of a way to draw up moisture. The tree dies a slow death, literally starved of water.

By combining the ongoing drought with the destruction caused by the bark beetle (which have killed millions of trees themselves), our beloved forest was ripe for disaster. Then, the spring wind began to blow. And, as it blew, it sucked any moisture from the ground that was left over from the meager snowfall of winter. With any luck, we could possibly make it through another fire season without a major conflagration. Our luck was soon to run out.

Chapter 2

Cibecue, Arizona is a White Mountain Apache village located, by road, approximately fifty miles from Show Low. As you drive off of the main highway and turn onto the two-lane blacktop leading into the village, you cross Cibecue Pass. From here you can look out over an expanse of forestland that encompasses not only the Apache Reservation, but also a vast part of the Apache-Sitgrieves National Forest. As you gaze over this breathtaking vista, you can make out swaths of land that seem a bit barren, a red dust chalk mark on an otherwise green background. This is where fire has visited the land. In some cases the fire was started intentionally for the purpose of clearing the underbrush in what use to be known as a "controlled burn." The term has since been changed to "prescribed burn." I guess it seems a more sterile, pharmaceutical term, as if there were a forest physician who, upon seeing a specific area of the forest, would recommend this procedure to benefit his patient. The change in terminology came about after some controlled burns by the U.S.D.A. Forest Service got out of control (the most notorious being the Cerro Grande Fire in New Mexico) and burned thousands upon thousands of acres of forest and hundreds of homes. Lightning may have caused other fires and some could have been human caused, such as an escaped campfire or a carelessly tossed cigarette. All are common causes of fire in the woods.

At the top of the pass are thousands of dead pine and oak trees, the remnants of a lightning-caused fire from a few years ago. The fire started in steep, rugged terrain and, before the fire crews could arrive, climbed up the canyon walls and burned a few thousand acres before being contained. This type of fire can be accepted. It was started by a naturally occurring phenomenon and, though the remains are unsightly, it is more easily understood than a human caused fire.

As you wind down the pass into Cibecue you begin seeing a change in vegetation. You rapidly descend through Ponderosa and spruce, to oak and pinion, to a wide-open range of grassland. Visible across the meadows is the village of Cibecue. The word Cibecue is really an English bastardization of the Apache term, "Dish'chii'bikoh," that describes the area where the village lies. It refers to the red bluff cliffs and green valley below. As you peer out across the grassy plain you see a swath of green from the cottonwood, willow and ash trees that line Cibecue Creek. In the distance, a large brown dome sits on a hill like a mushroom straight from the adventures of Alice in Wonderland. It houses the high school and seems remarkably out of place in this tiny hamlet.

Entering Cibecue, you get your first view of the stream that has sustained this settlement for hundreds of years. Towering cottonwood trees shade the stream and the few homes situated along its bank. On a hillside above the stream is an old sawmill with huge piles of sawdust drifting down from it. The sawdust and shavings get so thick that the Apache use a bulldozer to level it off and manage its bulk. I am a volunteer member of the Linden Fire Department and was once called upon to drive a water tender to this site when a fire broke out in the sawdust tailings. The fire was contained before it climbed the hill to the sawmill itself, but it smoldered underground in the shavings for months.

As you come to the northern end of Cibecue you pass over a bridge and continue on to the commerce center. This consists of a post office and a grocery store. There are a couple of gas pumps and, as a testament to modern technology, a cell phone company. The other businesses in town are a tire shop, a trading post, and a health center. The health services center is the reason I come to Cibecue on a daily basis. I pick up laboratory specimens there and, after picking up the specimens in Whiteriver (another town on the Apache Reservation), deliver them to Show Low to be picked up by another driver and taken to Phoenix. I am a visitor to Cibecue for only a few minutes a day. There are people who have spent their whole lives here.

It was on the outskirts of Cibecue, where something happened that would change the lives of countless people forever. It happened on June 18th, 2002. Or maybe it happened a hundred years ago. I can't speak to the social ramifications of life on a Reservation. I *can* speak to one of the consequences that arose from it.

Chapter 3

Out in the back of the village of Cibecue is an old rodeo arena. The Apache would have buck-outs, bull riding contests and bronc busting events here. It's called the Red Dust Arena because of the rust colored dirt found everywhere on this mountain. On a hot, windy June afternoon a young Apache man strode out into the grass beyond the rodeo grounds. I would think he was looking for a specific area. Dust would have kicked up from his boots as he walked through the parched grass and brush.

He was out of work. In the past, he had done contract firefighting for Fort Apache Fire Management, earning several dollars an hour for cutting lines around fires that had started for whatever reason. It was hard work. Using shovels or Pulaski's, the line was cut by scraping any burnable matter away from the fire. The idea is to cut off the fire's fuel, thus making management of the fire more attainable.

He was not alone. Hundreds of Apache have done this for many years. They have formed elite Hotshot crews whose firefighting abilities are recognized worldwide. The Apache have lived with fire for a long, long time. It is at once, their enemy and their friend. A fire that is too large can endanger not only their homes and villages, but also the stands of timber that feed the sawmills. A good fire is one that clears the underbrush, wipes out unwanted seedlings and keeps the forest healthy.

The Apache have been able to manage their forests relatively unencumbered by outside influences. In this age of the Sierra Club and Earth First! and the Environmental Liberation Front, who are notorious for filing lawsuits to prevent thinning and logging in the forest, the Apache have done a respectable job of managing their timber resources. To me, they have proven that logging and thinning the forest is not synonymous with the destruction of the forest.

There are many places where Reservation land butts up to private land. The difference between the two is astounding. On the Reservation side, the trees are widely spaced, growing at a rate of about fifty per acre. On the private and State managed lands, the trees are sickly and growing so close together that they are literally choking themselves to death. These so-called "dog hair" thickets are everywhere because of a policy adopted at the turn of the twentieth century that decreed all forest fires a hazard. A total fire-suppression attitude was put into place, and now, one hundred years later, we are seeing the result. The Apache, however, have thinned a good portion of their forest to pre-Columbus days, when the wooded areas were near park-like in their beauty.

The White Mountain Apache are inextricably linked to the forest. Their livelihood is completely dependant upon the welfare of the Ponderosa and spruce stands that are abundant across their Reservation. Be it from timber sales, hunting for the many big game animals on their land, fishing for trout in the lakes and streams or tourism dollars from people escaping the heat of Tucson and Phoenix, the forest is their lifeblood.

The young man in the back of the rodeo grounds, I think, knew this. It is in the blood of the Apache people to know this. It is known without being said. For the want of a job and a few dollars, this young man put aside this knowledge. He forgot what his ancestors have always known. As he looked up at the steep walls of the mountains behind the rodeo grounds and the brown, dry grass below… he forgot.

He lit a match and set fire to the grass. It took off immediately. Smoke began to curl up into the air as the fire crackled through the grass as if it were paper. This was not the first fire he had set today. He had put a match to another area that was closer to town. That, also, caught fire and began to spread. It got up to around a half an acre before it was spotted by the local fire crews and extinguished. The Pina Fire, as it was named, was contained at an acre. The fire personnel knew that an arsonist had set it. Now, here at the rodeo grounds, this new fire would be harder to spot. It would have a better chance to run and cover more acreage before anyone would be sent out to fight it.

As the fire began to grow, it moved into some low-lying brush and chaparral. This also caught fire immediately and added a new intensity to the flames. The fire began to get hotter and the flames went from a yellow color to orange. As the fire continued to run through the vegetation, smoke began to rise into the air. White at first, the smoke was now turning black. He was amazed at how fast the fire was moving compared to other fires he had set before (his family would say later that he was infatuated with fire when he was a young boy). Those other fires had moved much slower, as if the plants and trees were resisting it. But this fire was different. This time, it appeared that the grass and brush and trees were welcoming the flames, beckoning the fire to take them next. And as the fire obliged, it grew.

I think he would have begun to get scared. It was only a matter of time before the fire crews would arrive and he couldn't be here when that happened. He spun around and began to head back to Cibecue, turning his back on a fire that would change the lives of the White Mountain Apache for generations to come. And higher up, on the Mogollon Rim, which is a geographical feature dividing the low deserts from the mountain country, the people living in the many communities there had no idea what was in store for them.

Chapter 4

On the afternoon of June 18th, 2002, I was finishing up my route. I had collected the lab specimens from both Cibecue and Whiteriver and dropped them off at the collection point used by the other couriers with whom I work. I headed to the Show Low Municipal Airport to drop off the bank bags and boxes of blood I had picked up from some of my other stops. The airport sits a good deal higher than the city and affords a 360-degree view of the surrounding area. It is mostly flat, but you can see the Rim to the west and the high mesa land to the north. To the east are the mountains leading to Springerville and to the south lie the areas most popular with the tourists and residents. Here are the lakes and streams and the cooler temperatures that bring so many people from Tucson and Phoenix to the area.

As I looked off to the west I could see a column of smoke rising into the air. It was relatively small, but any smoke at all was a cause for concern at this time of year. When I was in Cibecue, earlier that afternoon, I had stopped at the trading post for a soda. Micki, who manages the post with her husband, David, told me that there had been a fire there that morning. I was certain that she told me it had been put out. But there it was. A plume of smoke, rising into the air, and it was coming from the direction of Cibecue. At 4:05 p.m. I called 911 on my cell phone to report it.

"911, what is your emergency?"

"Yes ma'am, I am calling to see if anyone has reported this column of smoke to the west of Show Low." The operator told me that it had not been reported. "This is going to be on the Reservation." I replied.

"Sir, Stay on the line and I will patch you through to Whiteriver."

Whiteriver is where the Fort Apache Fire Management offices are located. Through these offices, crews are dispatched to whatever fire emergency occurs. When the operator in Whiteriver answered, I again inquired about the smoke to the west of town.

"Yes sir, the fire is in Cibecue and Fire Management has it under control at this time."

Well, I'm no expert at wildfires. I have been on a couple of brush fires during my tenure with the volunteer fire department, but all in all I was pretty green when it came to the knowledge of fire behavior. I thanked the operator for the information and looked back at the ominous looking column on the horizon. In the short time I had been on the phone, this column had grown. It was not only going higher into the sky, but the smoke was getting darker. I knew that that was not a good sign. When smoke from a forest fire turns black, it means that it is getting into the juniper and, quite possibly, the Ponderosa pine.

From my vantage point at the airport, I could draw an imaginary line from the runway, to Linden, to the smoke. Not a good sign. Not a good sign, indeed. If that fire comes up the Rim, it's going to come into Linden. I recalled the words of the operator to whom I'd just spoken. It's under control. I remember thinking to myself, "If that's under control, I'd hate to see one that's out of control."

Not a good sign.

Indeed.

Chapter 5

My wife, Carol, and I had discussed the possibility of a wildfire occurring. It was the sort of conversation that you have when, although the topic is real and possible, you just don't think it could actually happen. We knew that the forest was extremely dry. In fact, as recently as two weeks ago, there had been a ten-acre forest fire fifteen miles south of Show Low. A motorist pulling off to the side of the road started that blaze. The catalytic converter on the undercarriage of the car brushed against the dry, foot tall grass and ignited it. It quickly spread and soon began running up into the small pine trees. Fire crews from Fort Apache and Show Low were dispatched immediately to quell the fire. We could see the smoke from our front porch.

In the distance, a small single engine air tanker (SEAT) could be seen flying over the area. These small, versatile planes are invaluable when it comes to firefighting. They can maneuver into areas that would take a ground crew hours to reach. The fire was knocked down quickly and a collective sigh of relief could be heard throughout the region. Had this situation not been attacked immediately, there was the very real possibility of flames running into the mountaintop communities a few miles away.

This brought home to Carol and me, the idea that a fire was not impossible. I remember the words of Linden Fire Chief Marilyn Price, during our training, that "it's not a matter of *if* but *when*" a fire will run through our communities on the mountain.

We have had wildland training exercises for many years. That's the nature of being on a rural, volunteer fire department. You train for whatever scenarios you can envision happening in your area. We have trained for barn fires and the unique problems that burning hay can present. We have also had haz-mat (hazardous material) training for several reasons. First and foremost is the idea that this is a rural farming and ranching area, and there is the likelihood of pesticides and fertilizers being involved in a fire. Another, more sinister aspect of our training, is the possibility of clandestine "meth-labs" being involved.

Because of the vast, open areas on this mountain, it is not uncommon to hear of the local police and Sheriff's deputies occasionally busting one of these operations. The chemicals involved in producing meth are a veritable laundry list of lethal and combustible ingredients.

There is also a major state highway that cuts through our town, and the possibility of a semi-truck overturning and dumping a hazardous load of material cannot be overlooked. But wildfire is the most glaring reason that we train. When you live in a forest, the thought of a wildfire lays in the back of your mind all the time, especially this time of year, when the wind can blow for months at a time. The combination of wind, drought, and fire is as combustible and lethal as a meth-lab. We trained for the hellish scenarios that we thought could never happen, that we hoped would never happen.

Carol and I decided that, to be on the safe side, we should take some precautions in the event of a fire. First, we went to the local Wal-Mart and purchased a small fire safe in which to put some of Carol's jewelry. We also gathered up our important papers and documents and placed them in a briefcase so as to be ready to grab at a moments notice. Finally, we planned different escape routes and made plans to get our animals to safety as best we could. You can plan for a thousand different situations, but you know that something will be forgotten. We did the best we could, not knowing if a fire would happen or from which direction it may come.

As I drove home to Linden from the airport I was already picking up a good bit of chatter on my fire radio regarding the plume of smoke outside of town. Apparently, Show Low Fire Department had headed in the direction of Cibecue but was turned back on the orders of the BIA (Bureau of Indian Affairs) and the Fort Apache Fire Management crews on the scene of the fire. This is peculiar, I remember thinking, because there is a standing mutual-aid order that is supposed to be put into effect whenever a fire threatens *any* community. I thought, at the time, that this was a good indication that the fire was, indeed, being contained and brought under control. However, the column of smoke continued to grow, becoming darker and more dense with each passing minute.

I called Carol, who, like myself, has her own courier route and was driving in from Springerville. I wanted to warn her of the sight awaiting her when she crossed the summit and was able to see the Linden valley. I was concerned about how she would react to the smoke on the horizon. I told her, calmly, everything that I was hearing about the fire. It was under control and Show Low Fire Department had been turned back. It should be over by this evening. As I was talking to her, I kept looking at the smoke column, hoping my tone of voice did not sound as hollow to her as it did to me.

I drove straight to the Linden Fire Department's main station to find out what they were hearing about the fire. I turned into the parking lot and could see that all of our firefighting apparatus was out of the bays and pointing toward the highway. The smoke, looming menacingly on the horizon, was visible from the front of the station. The fire personnel at the station had assumed, as had I, that all of the local fire departments would be called upon to send a crew and some type of firefighting equipment to Cibecue to aid in putting out this fire. I talked to Ryan Turner first.

Ryan, whom we had nicknamed "Nozzle", is a young, ambitious firefighter. He joined the department shortly after I did. As I approached him, I could see that his eyes, normally blue and clear, were clouded with concern over the fire to our south. I knew that he would be eager to go on a run to the Reservation and he was moving about the station, restlessly awaiting the go-ahead call for resources.

"Have we been called out yet, Nozzle?" I asked.

"Not yet," he replied. "They supposedly have a line around it, but I think that's bull. Look at that column!"

We both stood in the station parking lot gazing at the gray-black tower on the other side of the Rim.

It was obvious to us that this fire was far from being "under control." It was very much out of control and nobody could fathom why we hadn't been put on stand-by, at the very least. As he stared across the space of twenty miles, I could sense a foreboding about him. I knew he was gauging the location of the fire against the location of his home, which was situated in the Timberland Acres subdivision in Linden.

Timberland Acres, or simply T/A as the locals refer to it, is situated in a rugged, hilly part of Linden known as Juniper Ridge. There are approximately three hundred homes in this area. Unless you live in T/A, it can seem like a maze if you are trying to get from one place to another. There is a somewhat circular road that winds around the perimeter with dozens of other roads that intersect in the center of the circle. The main problem with this street system is the fact that a single blacktop road, much like a balloon on a string, accesses the circular roadway. There is one way in and one way out. This is not much of a problem in years when we have received significant rain and snowfall but in a drought situation, such as we find ourselves in now, it becomes a concern. Fighting a fire in Timberland Acres is a scenario that we have trained for. There are fire hydrants in a few locations inside the neighborhood, but we all knew, though it was unspoken, that if a fire got loose in T/A, all we could hope for would be to get everyone out safely

The homes in Timberland Acres consist of many cabins and summer homes, but there are an increasing number of people who have chosen to live here full-time. Because the area is slightly higher in elevation, the winters are a bit more harsh, the snowfall (when we get it) a bit deeper and the temperatures a bit cooler than the rest of Linden. The forest in this area is dense. There are homes built in areas which seem to be in perpetual dusk, because the trees are so thick. Along with the pine, there are a number of huge Alligator junipers, so-named because their bark resembles an alligator hide, and a mix of oak and pinion. After a summer rainstorm, this area is fragrant with the scent of the different trees. Hummingbirds, by the thousands, spend their summer here. There are also javelina, cougar, raccoon, squirrel, rabbit, deer, elk and, occasionally, black bear that call this area home.

I turned my gaze from the foothills of T/A. Other fire department personnel began showing up for the same reason that I had pulled in. Everyone wanted to know about the smoke.

Because we hadn't been called out to help with the fire in Cibecue, there was not much we could do but go home. Our radios are equipped with a page-out feature, so the county dispatcher could send out a tone and a message if we were going to be called upon to help.

I left the department with an uneasy feeling. Something didn't seem right about this whole damn deal. The ten-acre fire of a few weeks ago was jumped upon with what could be considered over-kill, but they were letting this one burn. And burn it was. The plume had nearly doubled in size since I had called 911. That was an hour and a half ago.

I pulled into my driveway to see Carol out watering the trees and grass in our yard. Our water bill had been pretty high the last couple of months because we were trying to do what nature had been unable to do. That is, supply our trees with the moisture needed to stay alive. I'm not sure that we could ever water enough to compensate for the lack of rain and snow, but we were trying. I told Carol that I had heard no new information, and we would just have to wait to see what would happen.

As we talked in the front yard, I noticed what appeared to be snow wafting down from the sky. It was, actually, quite pretty, but I knew what it was. Ash. I walked over to where one particularly large piece had fallen and was able to make out the shape of an oak leaf. This meant that the fire was definitely burning into the scrub and was burning with an intensity that was hot enough to send this bit of ash over twenty air miles to the north.

We went into the house, put the jewelry in the fire safe and pulled the briefcase from under the desk, just in case we got an order to go. I didn't think that would happen, but we would be prepared if such an order did come down. At around 7:00 p.m. the phone rang. It was Nozzle. "I just heard that the fire jumped the line. They've lost it, man," he told me, in a calm, dispassionate voice. "They've lost it."

Chapter 6

I awoke early the next day. It was 4:30 a.m. when I quietly closed our bedroom door so I wouldn't disturb Carol. After a night of fitful dreams about smoke and ash, I was ready to get out of bed. My first thoughts were about the fire and what had occurred overnight.

A thin line of dim light on the horizon separated night from day as I stepped out on the front porch. The smell of smoke hung in the morning air and a hazy, blue fog shrouded my neighborhood. As daylight began breaking, I scanned the skyline to the south to see if the column of smoke, so stark and menacing yesterday evening, was visible. It was not. What I didn't know at that time was that fire will "lay down" at night, hampered in its progress by cooler temperatures and higher, nighttime humidity. This gave me a sense of hope that they had been able to regain the upper hand on this fire.

I made a pot of coffee, poured myself a cup and sat on the front porch scanning the sky to the south. As the morning light grew brighter I could see that the ash-fall from last night had left gray drifts at the base of the trees and in the corners of the porch. It must have become heavier after we went to bed. If I used my imagination I could envision this as a light snowfall, dusting the ground and the branches of the trees. The acrid smell of smoke, however, shattered this brief illusion. I looked across the road toward my neighbors' house and could see that the smoke in the air had reduced visibility to about a mile, maybe less. I knew Dewayne was not working today and hoped I would see him in his yard doing some early watering. He has had a good deal of wildland firefighting training, and I was anxious to get his opinion on the way the fire looked this morning. I saw no movement, however, so I turned on the television to see if the Phoenix news had picked up on this story.

We were locked in an informational vacuum. I couldn't believe that there was so little detail coming out about this fire, when it obviously was, or had been, burning ferociously. I decided that I would go back to the fire station after breakfast to see if any new information had been released. After showering and putting some bacon on the stove, the phone rang. It was my dad. He and his wife Anna had been planning to come up from Tucson this coming weekend to stay for a few days. He was calling to let me know when they would be leaving Tucson and when they would arrive in Linden. I told him that he might want to put the trip on hold. "We've got a pretty big fire up here, Dad." I could tell by his response that this was the first he had heard about the fire, which meant that the news media in Phoenix *and* Tucson hadn't picked up the story yet. I told him I would call and update him when I heard more.

I ate breakfast and went to the station. A number of Navajo County Sheriff's Department vehicles were in the parking lot as well as a few police vehicles from Show Low. There was obviously some sort of discussion going on regarding the fire. Several Linden Fire personnel were milling about the station, drinking coffee and occasionally looking out across the parking lot at the column of smoke, which had begun to rise up into the sky again. The definitive word was that the fire had, indeed, jumped the line that had, allegedly, been cut around it. From what I could gather, it sounded more likely that they had tried to use some of the natural barriers to act as a fire line rather than actually cutting a line by hand or with a bulldozer. Cibecue Creek was one of the barriers they had planned on using, but the fire had apparently jumped the stream and was now starting to burn into a canyon and up through one of the many draws leading to the Rim.

The police and Sheriff's officials were meeting with Chief Price in her office upstairs. The topic was evacuation. At that time, it was unclear what area they were talking about evacuating. Some of the firefighters at the station had pulled out a Forest Service map and were trying to pinpoint the location of the fire based on the few coordinates we had heard. After studying the map, we came to the conclusion that the communities of Pinedale and Clay Springs, which are about ten miles west of Linden, appeared to be the likely candidates.

We were beginning to hear more about the personnel and equipment in place on the Reservation, but the numbers varied every time we heard them. Two hundred plus firefighters, three bulldozers and two SEATS were the first estimates I heard. The question in everyone's mind was: how could they lose the fire line with that many resources? The fire had laid down last night. Couldn't they have dozed a line around it then? What in hell were they doing all night? There were a million questions and no answers.

Across the highway and down at the base of the Mogollon Rim, the fire was waking up. It was just beginning to stretch and yawn. But it was awake and ready to move. Ash was once again floating down from the sky and the wind was starting to pick up. I could feel a sense of urgency in the department. Let's get a plan in place, guys! We waited to get word from the brass upstairs. So far, we were hearing nothing.

I sat at a table inside the station drinking coffee. The whole situation seemed somewhat surreal. I should be at home, finishing up the breakfast dishes and getting ready to do some work in the garden, but here I am at the Linden Fire main station, waiting on a possible evacuation notice. I tried to remember what documents we had put into the briefcase and what jewelry Carol had locked away in the safe. I wondered if I should call her but decided that there would be no point in alarming her unnecessarily. Maybe the smoke is from a back burn, lit to ward off the fires advance up the rim. I ran through many different scenarios in my head to try and explain away the grotesque smoke cloud looming on the horizon, but every explanation seemed hollow. It was there. It was very real and we were going to have to deal with it. Soon.

We could hear muffled voices from the meeting room upstairs and tried to glean what information we could from them. Someone thought they had heard that only Pinedale would be evacuated. That made sense to me because when I looked at the Forest Service map, Pinedale seemed to be in the crosshairs, judging from the way the wind was blowing today. But summer winds can be fickle, blowing from one direction and then abruptly shifting and blowing from another. I remember thinking that I wouldn't want to be the one who made this call. Most of the folks living in this area have been here for a long time. They will not take kindly to being told to leave their homes. If they are forced to evacuate and the fire is put under control, there will be hell to pay down the road.

All of a sudden, there was a commotion from upstairs. People were coming down the stairwell rather quickly.

"OK, I'll alert my people, lets get it going," I heard someone say.

As Chief Price came down the stairs, the look on her face told me all I needed to know. The evacuation order had been given for Pinedale, Clay Springs *and* Linden. Everyone was going to be told to go to the gym at the Show Low High School. The personnel at the department were hurriedly trying to formulate a plan as to how to get the word out to the community. My neighbor, Dewayne Saxton, arrived at the firehouse and was preparing to take one of our brush trucks out to Timberland Acres. They would use a bullhorn to alert the people out there to the evacuation.

I took advantage of this moment and ran to my truck and drove home. I had a knot in my stomach as I turned onto my road. I did not want to tell Carol about the order to evacuate. But she had to know and if I told her now, she would have a head start on the rest of Linden. I knew the highway would be jammed soon and wanted to get her and our cats out of here.

I practically slid into our driveway, kicking up gravel and dust! I remember thinking, "Damn it! I should slow down. She's going to be freaked out as it is. I don't need to come in here like a storm trooper and add to the anxiety." I parked the truck and walked up to the porch. Carol met me at the door with a look of apprehension on her face.

"They're evacuating Linden. You've got to get going," I told her.

"Oh my God, not Linden," she replied. "Where am I supposed to go?"

"They're telling everyone to go to the high school gym. Just go there and wait until someone tells you what to do next."

Carol backed her Honda Accord up to the front porch and we began loading the trunk with the briefcase and things that we had prepared earlier. My mind was racing, trying to think of what else she might need. I went to our shed and grabbed a couple of sleeping bags and a three-man tent.

"We need to get the cats, honey. Do you know where they are?" I asked.

"They're all inside the house. I'm going to need the pet carrier. What am I supposed to do with them at the school? I can't leave them in the car all the time. It's too hot," she replied.

I could tell that the stress was already mounting inside of her.

"Carol, I don't know. You'll just have to play it by ear until you see what's going on at the gym. Right now, we have to get you out of here or else you'll be stuck on the highway for who knows how long. Just get the cats' food and some clothes for yourself and get going. I'll call you on your cell phone as soon as I hear something."

I was getting rather edgy myself. I wanted to be able to tell her exactly what to do and where to go and that everything would be fine. But this was a situation that neither of us had experienced and, quite frankly, never expected to experience.

We packed what we could into the Honda. We put Coco, our Chocolate Point Siamese, into the pet carrier. She was the most shy and temperamental of our three cats and we were afraid that if she somehow got out of the car in Show Low, we would never see her again. Xena, our Lilac Point Siamese, had ridden in the car numerous times and would not be as apt to jump out, and Tigger, a precocious Ocicat, was very young and would more than likely ride on Carol's lap for the trip into town.

After loading everything we could think of into the car, Carol turned towards me. She had tears in her eyes. I hugged her and gave her a kiss.

"Look sweetie, I think they're doing this mostly as a precaution. You'll probably have to spend the night at the school until they see what the fire is going to do and then you'll be able to come home. I'll call you as soon as I can," I told her, as reassuringly as I could.

"What about you? Are you going to stay here?" she asked.

"I'm not sure what we're going to do. They want all Linden Fire personnel at the station. I just don't know right now. I'm sure they'll tell us something when I get back there. Now get going and I'll call you as soon as I can," I replied.

The tears were still on her cheek as I kissed her and told her that I loved her.

"I love you too. Please be careful. Don't let our home burn."

It was almost a plea and it tugged at my heart. I wanted to get into the car and go with her to the school, to make sure she would be safe, but I had to stay in Linden and we both knew it.

I stood in the driveway and watched the Honda drive down our dusty road. When it was out of sight, I went to the house and locked the doors. All of the windows were closed because we had the air-conditioner on. I left it that way, thinking that if I were able to come home tonight I would shut it off then. Perhaps the closed windows would keep the smell of smoke out of the house for a while.

I got back in my Isuzu Trooper and headed towards the fire department. On the way, I saw one of my neighbors standing in his front yard. I stopped and told him that an evacuation order had been given. If he left now, he would have a head start on the rest of the community. Honestly, I don't know that he believed me, but he thanked me anyway. When I reached Highway 260 I could see a line of traffic beginning to form already, and it was headed toward Show

Low. Obviously, people were beginning to heed the order to evacuate.

Making a right turn, away from Show Low, I started driving to the station. So many thoughts were going through my mind. Was the evacuation really necessary? Isn't the fire still several miles away? Will Carol be able to manage the three cats in a strange environment by herself? Will we be able to put this fire out?

Chapter 7

As I was locking up the house, Carol was turning left onto Highway 260 going toward Show Low. The road makes a sweeping curve to the southeast, while gradually climbing up Joe Tank Hill. There is a road at the crest of the hill named, appropriately, Joe Tank Road. A stock pond off of this road lends its name to both the road and the hill. As you round this curve, it tends to throw off your sense of direction. While you think you may be traveling in an easterly direction, you are actually traveling south. It's a phenomenon that I thought was, most likely, unique to myself, until I found out that people who have lived here much longer than I, have had the same perception. I first noticed this during the summer monsoon season. As I would run my courier route I would see the afternoon storms building and try to guess how close they were to Linden. The storms that I thought should be on top of the area would always turn out to be either north or east or south of Linden.

This directional incongruity would contribute to the tale of the "Linden Bubble," an invisible dome of air, of which the most severe thunderstorm cannot penetrate. In the summer rainy season, the sky to our east and south will turn black and foreboding with lightning flashing and thunder rumbling. I would stand still and try to track the movement of the clouds. Usually they are moving in our direction because of the clockwise circulation of a gigantic high-pressure system that parks itself over the Four Corners area of the southwest. As the storms approach the Linden valley, they will, quite literally, split and go either north or south of us. This is not an occasional occurrence and will actually happen more often than not. Hell, this happens nearly all of the time. While the city of Show Low, a mere mile and a half away, can get an absolute drenching, the highway through Linden will be dry. Now, I'm not sure if there is some geographic anomaly that creates this feat of magically disappearing rainstorms, but it is a real and time-tested event. I cannot adequately express the feeling of being left high and dry, wishing only for enough rain to soak your garden or lawn, and to be denied, all the while knowing that rainwater is flowing through the streets of Show Low. It's akin to being jilted by a lover. That's about as close as I can get to describe it.

As Carol made her way up Joe Tank Hill, the column of smoke appeared to shift and follow her direction of travel, making it seem as if the fire were just outside of town. As she came into the city limits, she turned left onto Old Linden Road and headed toward Show Low High School. A line of cars and trucks was beginning to form behind her as other folks meandered toward the school, none knowing what to expect or who to talk to when they got there. She pulled into the parking lot, trying to find out where she was supposed to go. No one seemed to have any information about the school becoming a shelter. There were no policemen to ask, there were no city officials to ask, and there were no school officials to ask, either. There was, however, a bunch of people who, like herself, had been told to evacuate to the gymnasium at the school. She parked the car and got out.

"Is this where we're supposed to go?" she asked. The group of people that were milling about were as confused as she.

"I don't know. I'm not from around here," someone replied.

"Shouldn't there be someone here to let us know what's going on?" someone else inquired.

"I just heard on the radio that they're saying we're supposed to go to Springerville now," another person replied.

With no one seemingly in command or acting in an official capacity at the school, Carol assumed that she should start driving to Springerville, some fifty miles away.

She got back onto Old Linden Road and proceeded toward downtown Show Low. Steve Bower, a friend whom I have known since we we're kids in Tucson, has a real estate office that Carol would have to drive right by. Seeing his truck parked in the lot of the office, she decided to stop in and let him know what was happening in Linden. Upon hearing of the evacuation and Carol's impending trip to Springerville he told her, "You're staying right here with me." Carol, thankful for the suggestion, agreed. She did not want to go all the way to Apache County to find a situation such as she found at the Show Low High School. She wanted to call and tell me where she was but could not get through on her cell phone. By this time the phones were in absolute gridlock with people calling each other. Traffic was beginning to flow down the Main Street of Show Low, known as the Deuce of Clubs (or simply, the Deuce, by locals), as word of the evacuation began spreading.

Steve had been working on a house in the community of White Mountain Lake, a modest subdivision that is several miles outside of the area slated for evacuation. He had been cleaning it up and selling some of the household items left behind by the previous owner. Making a quick decision, Steve told Carol that they could all stay there in the event that Show Low was to be evacuated also. They would be joined by Steve's fiancée, Cindy, who worked at the Navapache Regional Medical Center and was probably aware of what was going on in Linden and Pinedale. The house was rather small, but could

Photos by Tim Heim

This sequence of photos was taken from Gentry Lookout beginning at approximately 4:00pm

Gary Phillip Holdcroft

Photos by Tim Heim

and ending at approximately 6:30pm on June 18th, 2002. The Rodeo Fire was underway.

.

Gary Phillip Holdcroft

accommodate the three of them (and our cats) until they would be allowed to return home. Carol was very grateful for this generous offer because, at the very least, it gave her some sense of a plan. She would not have to go into Springerville, not knowing where to go or what to do once she arrived.

Carol waited in Steve's office while he finished up the business on which he was working. Because it was so hot outside, she brought the cats into the air-conditioned office one at a time to let them cool off. This was going to be hard on the cats, but she was trying as best she could to keep them calm and safe.

Unaware of any of this, I was on my way to the Linden Fire Department to see what we were going to do about this fire. There's an old saying among firefighters: "You put the wet stuff on the red stuff." I hoped that that was going to be all it took.

Chapter 8

I pulled into the parking lot at the department not knowing what to expect, noticing that all three bay doors were open and that most of our trucks were gone. We had recently acquired a brand new "attack" engine that was equipped with the latest fire fighting technology. It had a CAF (compressed air and foam) system on it and was small and maneuverable. It was gone, as well as our brush truck and a support vehicle, one we had christened "Rescue." I knew that they were being used to spread the word through the community that the evacuation was in effect and people had to get out. Now.

I felt more at ease knowing that Carol had missed most of this traffic, which, by now, was becoming bumper to bumper on Highway 260. It was amazing to see how much "stuff" people had been able to load onto their pick-up trucks and car tops. How had they decided what was to go and what was to stay? Apparently, some folks were taking this situation very seriously. Their vehicles were so over-loaded that it appeared as though they were moving to another state. Others seemed to be taking the situation as merely an inconvenience. They had little or nothing in their cars and trucks and would glance over at the fire department as they went by, as if it were Linden Fire, alone, that called for the evacuation. Oh well. What was important was that they were leaving. The people in the communities of Pinedale and Clay Springs were undergoing their own evacuation and while some were going to Show Low, others decided to go to the town of Heber-Overgaard, which is approximately twenty miles away.

Heber-Overgaard is a picturesque little town, built up along Highway 260, and is home to many full time residents. The majority of the homes in the many trailer parks, however, are summer homes and getaways for residents of Tucson and Phoenix. A few motels and restaurants there, as well as convenience stores and curiosity shops, complete the town. It would be able to accommodate a good many of the evacuees for several days, if necessary.

Traffic was flowing smoothly despite the heavy volume and it did not appear that traffic control would be needed. I could see Engine 2, which is normally housed at the Timberland Acres sub-station, approaching the Linden Fire main station. Capt. Bob Filley was manning it. He backed the engine up to one of the bays that normally held a brush truck and got out.

Bob is a thin, rather lanky gentleman who, I would guess, is approaching his sixties. He's been on the fire department for many years. A man of few words, he is very knowledgeable about firefighting procedures and equipment but has also been a deputy sheriff, an animal control officer *and* he holds a pilots license, as well. He and I walked into the main room of the department at about the same time. Up until that time, I had never really spoken in depth with Bob. We would attend the bi-monthly classes and perhaps even train together, but there was not much conversation otherwise.

The firehouse was fairly quiet considering the mass exodus taking place just outside. However, the phone was ringing off the hook. Frightened residents were calling to confirm that an evacuation was in effect or asking what they should do with their pets and did they *really* have to go?

Bob and I were dressed the same. We had recently been issued bright, orange jumpsuits (exactly like the federal prisoners wear!) with the word "Rescue" written down the sleeve and leg in reflective lettering, and the Linden Fire logo on the back. Bob was pacing slowly around the room with his hands in his pockets. We could hear on our radios that nearly all of Linden had been notified of the need to depart and it was now pretty much up to the Sheriff's department to flush out anyone that hadn't been told or simply wouldn't leave.

We sat at the station for an hour or so, waiting for some type of orders. At around 3:00 p.m. Chief Price instructed Bob and me to take Engine 2 out to Pinedale. By this time, equipment from some of the local fire departments was being sent in that direction. Most of the Linden Fire Department's equipment was already in Pinedale or on its way. Engine 3 had a full crew and was *staging*, meaning they were staying in one spot while awaiting further instructions, somewhere towards the back of Pinedale. Brush 702 was also staged near the area where the National Forest butted up to private land.

Chapter 9

As you enter Pinedale, you can't help but notice a quaint, covered, wooden bridge. The only one of its kind in Arizona, it lends a certain charm to the town. I could imagine this bridge in the winter. Snow covered, with horse drawn sleds traversing it, it would have a Currier and Ives appeal. However, on this late afternoon, it serves only as a means of transporting fire equipment into the area where the officials feel the fire is most likely to come. As the afternoon temperatures cool, the smoke is beginning to settle into the low-lying areas of the town. A fire hydrant is close to the covered bridge, and as we approached we could see an engine from a local unit filling its tank. We stopped and helped them roll up their hydrant lines and asked where the command center was located.

Before we could get an answer, Pinedale Fire Chief Sid Howard pulled up. He saw that we were from Linden and approached us immediately. "OK guys, I'm going to need you down the street at the other hydrant. We're going to be bringing the water tenders down here to fill up. Your job will be to see that they are filled and sent back to the line. Got it?"

Sid, a tall, sturdy looking fellow in his early sixties with a shock of gray-black hair poking out from his Pinedale-Clay Springs fire cap, looked somewhat tired. I was sure that he had been very busy trying to coordinate the resources that were rolling into town. It was not as though this was a first for him. Three years earlier, lightning had sparked off a fire on the outskirts of Pinedale. That fire had burned several hundred acres and came dangerously close to a group of homes that housed many full time residents and a community of artisans. The Cottonwood Fire, as it was named, also required a large amount of equipment and personnel to be managed and I'm sure that he was instrumental in the coordination of resources during that fire.

We followed Sid to the hydrant, which was a couple of blocks on the other side of the bridge and fifty feet up a side street. While Bob and Sid discussed what type of hose connections would be best suited for filling the tenders, I began pulling the large, yellow hydrant line off of the truck. We connected the hose to the fireplug and then to the engine and ran a two and a half inch hose in a loop down the street and then back to the truck. As the water tenders came in for a refill we would be able to fill them and send them back to the line in short order. After inspecting the connections, Sid left us and drove off to the back of town, where the smoke column was still very visible.

Within fifteen minutes, the first water tender came in to be filled. "How's it going back there?" Bob asked the driver.

"OK. Not much we can do but wait, at this point," he replied. He explained that they had been using this tender to wet down the main road so the dust wouldn't choke the firefighters who were staged in the area.

We topped of the large tank on the water tender and awaited the next one. I was expecting that we would have a continuous line of trucks coming in but that was the only one we would see.

I began looking around. Pinedale has an eclectic mix of homes. Some houses are built of red brick and have a mid-western feel about them, while others are obviously built from logs and boards and other materials supplied locally. Many homes are built from black cinder rock, which is everywhere on the mountain. A good many new homes are also being built in the area, and these homes tend to stick out, looking out of place amongst the older style construction that makes up most of Pinedale. Across the street sits a wide meadow. In the center is an old, red barn with several fences surrounding it. There was a chestnut mare still in one of the corrals and she was whinnying and pacing about the stall. I wondered if anyone was aware of this horse being here. The barn door was open and she could disappear inside. I made a mental note to bring this to someone's attention. Though I was not quite sure who would be in charge of livestock, the thought of this old mare being left alone in the smoke and ash didn't sit well with me.

Bob and I sat on the back of the engine, waiting for the next water tender to arrive. The afternoon was turning into evening and neither of had had anything to eat since breakfast. "Damn, I wonder if they're planning on feeding us?" Bob asked.

"That's a good question. I'm getting hungry," I replied. "I don't suppose there's going to be a roach coach rolling through here any time soon."

Bob dug through the cab of the engine but could only come up with some bottles of Gator-Aide.

"Well, at least we won't die of thirst. Starvation, maybe. But not thirst," he joked.

We laughed and began to regale each other with stories to pass the time. We still had not seen another water tender.

As we sat on the bumper of Engine 2, we would, occasionally, see a vehicle come down the road. Some were folks who had been allowed back into the area to load their livestock onto their trailers and others were stragglers who had been taking their sweet time to load up and get out. There was noticeably more law enforcement vehicles moving about, and I assumed they were checking the neighborhood to make sure everyone had moved into the safety zone. I hadn't seen anyone at the barn across the road and wondered how the horse was doing. The smoke in the air was starting to get thick and I hadn't heard any noise from the barn in quite a while. I've got to remember to tell someone about her.

At around 9:00 p.m. a truck pulled up behind the engine. We couldn't tell who it was because of the glare from the headlights, but I heard a voice and recognized it as Eva Dickinson, an EMT with Linden Fire. She was holding two brown lunch sacks out of the window of the pick-up truck. Bob and I thanked her for remembering us and sat back down on the bumper to eat. It was not much, a bologna sandwich, some potato chips and an apple, but it would ease the pangs of hunger. I ate the sandwich and chips but I saved most of the apple to give to the horse across the road. A little while later, an ambulance pulled up with some Jack-in-the-Box hamburgers. Now this was more like it!

The ambulance left and soon after, another vehicle came around the corner and stopped. It was a Forest Service truck. A young woman got out and introduced herself to us. I don't remember her name, but she told us that she lived just down the street and had come by to check on her home. The fire was a long distance away, but still, she wanted to make sure the windows were closed to keep the smoke from coming inside her house. She said that we were welcome to use the restroom and even shower if we wanted to. Thanking her for her kindness, we declined the offer. We promised to keep an eye on her place for as long as we were here. She drove away, hopefully knowing we would do our best.

It was after 10:00 p.m. now, so Bob pulled two cots from a storage bin on the engine. It would feel good to stretch out because the bumper of the engine was just not made to be a couch. I lay down and looked up at a half-moon in the sky. There appeared to be clouds drifting across the face of the crescent moon, sometimes fully obscuring the view, but I knew it was smoke. I heard a rustling noise from Bob's cot and looked over that way. He was standing. "Oh brother, look at that," he said.

I stood up to see what he was talking about. Towards the end of the street, we could see an orange glow through the trees. The glow was approximately ninety degrees from where we had been seeing the main column of smoke earlier.

"Man, it looks like the fire has split or something," I remarked. "I thought it was over there." I pointed in the direction of where the smoke had been.

"I dunno," Bob replied, "but that can't be good."

Not a good sign, indeed.

I lay back down for a while, trying to get a few moments sleep but my eyes kept going back to the horizon and the bright orange glow. Occasionally, it would die down and appear to be gone, only to reappear with a renewed vigor a moment later. There was no way I was going to be able to sleep.

I was reminded of a time at Big Lake when Carol and I were camping in a tent. The first night there, we slept like babies. The next morning, the park ranger came by to collect the money for the campsite and informed us that there had been a bear and her cub running through our camp area a day earlier. That evening, around a campfire, every little noise in the woods caused us to snap our heads in that direction. I don't think we slept for more than a couple of hours over the next two days. Now, I have a different "bear" prowling around. I think this one is more dangerous.

Chapter 10

The smoke began to grow more dense with each passing moment. I took off my Linden Fire cap and placed it over my mouth and nose to filter out as much smoke as possible. It helped somewhat (now the smoke smelled like sweat), but I could not even think about sleeping. I knew that Bob was awake and probably feeling the same way as I. We would much rather be *doing* something as opposed to just lying around. As the time approached 11:00 p.m. another vehicle pulled up and stopped at our location. It was Chief Howard.

"Alright guys," he said "I've got something for you to do. You can leave your hydrant line here and follow me up to the station."

We hurriedly disconnected our two and a half inch lines and stashed them in the compartments on the engine. Putting the old engine in gear, we followed Sid to the Pinedale main station. It felt good to be in motion. Time had been starting to drag while we were on the cots.

We pulled up in front of the station, which is an old Quonset style hut, consisting of a room for an engine and a water tender, a restroom, and an office. That was it. There was an engine ahead of us and I could make out the "White Mountain Lakes Fire" logo on the door. We were starting to get resources from all over the mountain now. A young man and a young woman stepped out of the engine and walked into the station. Bob and I followed them inside. Seeing a pot of coffee, I helped myself to a cup. It was a thick, nasty brew that looked like used motor oil. Just the way I like it!

The bay doors were wide open and I could see five or six other firefighters inside the steel dome. One of them was a rather husky fellow named Charlie Brown. I had met Charlie a few times before. His appearance is, initially, somewhat intimidating. His head is (I believe) shaved, and his general, overall look is that of a biker. After you get past the external Charlie Brown and actually exchange a few words with him, you find him to be a very funny man, with a compassionate, caring side. He was talking to Sid as Bob and I walked into the station. "Who would've thought it would be us two times in a row, huh Sid?" he asked, referring to the Cottonwood fire of a couple of years ago.

"I know Charlie," Sid replied softly. "You just never know what the good Lord has planned for you, do you?" I could tell that both of them were tired. This, however, was their home, their neighbors, their families and friends. They were going to fight this fire tooth and nail.

Sid had, obviously, been working on some type of plan. He assigned a certain section of a neighborhood to the White Mountain Lakes unit and asked Bob and me to follow him to our soon to be assigned location.

Neither Bob nor I were terribly familiar with all of the roads and side roads in Pinedale. After driving through the main section of town, we left the pavement and drove about three miles down a dusty, dirt road. This route would eventually lead you onto Forest Service land, and into some of the most scenic areas I have ever seen, should you choose to go that far. We turned right onto a more narrow road. The partially obscured street sign read "Danish Hollow Road," which was rough and bumpy and doglegged around for about a mile and a half, until we came to a house at the end. "This is a dead end road," I told Bob. "I don't know that I like this too much."

"I know," Bob replied. "Let's get back here and see what we've got." We waited for Sid to park and get out of his vehicle before we parked the engine alongside of him. "I want you guys to do structure protection out here. I don't think the fire will run through this particular area, but we'll keep you here just in case. I'll check on you later but you two keep your eyes open and get out of here if you have to," Sid told us. The tone of his voice was almost fatherly and reflected a genuine concern for our well-being. I didn't want to be the one who told Sid that we would, indeed, leave if we saw flames, and we would probably be leaving at a pretty quick pace. I looked at Bob and could tell he was thinking along similar lines. He looked at me and cocked an eyebrow. I nearly busted out laughing.

Chief Howard drove off in his pick-up truck. We waited until his taillights were out of sight before beginning an assessment of our surroundings. The house at the end of Danish Hollow Road was a three-bedroom manufactured home. Set on sloping land, which allowed for a large storage area under the house, it was faced with a terraced patio and porch on the front. A large storage shed on the property, as well as many appliances, were in various stages of disrepair. The five acres of land on which the house sat, were so thick with pine and oak trees that you could barely walk through them.

We meandered around trying to formulate a plan of attack, but were really just glad to be in a different location. I saw a door that led to the storage area under the house, unlatched it and peered in. I could not believe what I was seeing. Inside were dozens of cans of paint (some were five gallon containers), paint thinner, white gas for camp stoves, cans of spray paint and an array of other highly flammable materials. I called Bob over to have a look.

"Oh yeah, that's a great idea. Let's store all of our flammables under the house. What are these people thinking?" he said.

The more that we looked around, the more obvious it became that there would be very little we could do to defend this place. We could spray a layer of foam on the house and get out. That's about it. As we continued our assessment I saw some movement near the house. I walked over in time to see an old, gray cat run around the corner. I can't understand how somebody could leave a pet behind. My cats are an important part of my family. I hoped that it was a matter of them not being able to find their pet when they left as opposed to simply abandoning the poor animal.

Bob and I got back into the cab of Engine 2 and unwrapped the Jack-in-the-Box hamburgers and fries delivered to us earlier. The burgers were ice cold by now and the fries were hard little sticks. Glancing toward the house, I saw the gray cat peering over at us, only his head and front paws being visible. "Here kitty, kitty," I called. "I've got some french fries for you." I pitched a few fries in his direction and he promptly ran away. A few minutes later, however, he was sniffing at the fries and then looking back toward the engine. I should've known he wouldn't be interested in those hard, little twigs. Not being terribly hungry myself, and finding the hamburger less than appealing, I removed the patty and tossed it over towards the cat. Apparently, that was more to his liking because he snatched it up in his mouth and disappeared around the corner of the house. Sadly, that was the last I saw of him.

As we sat in the cab of the old fire engine, a red pick-up truck pulled up in front of the house. Driving the vehicle was Mel Epps, the Heber-Overgaard fire chief. He had come out to check on us. Getting tired, I wanted to catch a nap in the front the engine. Bob stepped out of the cab and walked over to Mel's truck. I decided to try and stretch out on the front porch of the house. I had spied a chaise-lounge on the deck and figured it would be more comfortable than the front seat of Engine 2. I laid down, put my hat over my face and tried to sleep, occasionally looking over towards Mel's truck.

Bob was leaning up against it, his arm slung over the cab, and he and Mel were talking. The smoke, by now, was so dense that I could barely make out the truck. The orange glow on the horizon still lingered, and I could hear a bulldozer droning and clanking in the distance. They were trying to cut a fire line somewhere close by. That meant that someone was concerned about the fire possibly running into this area, a thought that did not lend itself to one being able to sleep. I lay there, listening to the dozer, thinking about where we were: a dead end road with a power line running right through the middle of it, a fire burning to our south, and orders to try and protect a house that would be nearly impossible to save. I was wondering if, perhaps, we should take the engine back to the Pinedale main station to see if Sid would rethink our assignment.

Hearing another vehicle pulling up to the house, I glanced over to see Sid getting out. He walked over to Bob and Mel and had a few words with them. I put my hat back on and started towards them only to see the conversation break up and both Sid and Mel drive off. "They want us to go back to the Pinedale station," Bob told me. "I guess they think this is too dangerous." This was fine with me. I had come to that same conclusion a few hours ago.

Dawn was beginning to light the eastern sky, the dim light diffused by the thick smoke. We loaded ourselves into

Engine 2 and started pulling out of the semi-circular driveway. I looked back towards the house to see if I could spot the charcoal-gray feline. There was no sign of him. "Good luck to you, old cat," I thought to myself. "Good luck."

Chapter 11

The morning was getting brighter by the minute as we parked down the street from the Pinedale station. There were several other fire trucks there and I assumed that a new plan had been formulated. Someone had been able to get some doughnuts into the station, so I helped myself to two and another cup of the hideously strong coffee from last night. As the day began to get brighter, I could feel the weariness begin to subside a bit.

The department was subdued, with not a whole lot of conversation. I could see a map pinned to the wall with a red circle just below Pinedale. The fire had grown overnight. The last estimate I had heard was two, possibly three hundred acres but this morning they were talking about several thousand acres being consumed and the day was just beginning.

Sid called Bob and me over to the front of the Quonset hut. He, like the rest of the males, was now sporting a stubbly beard and bloodshot eyes from the lack of sleep. He pointed across the meadow behind the firehouse. "I'm going to have you guys set up at that house there," he said. "There are lookouts sitting up on the house above town. When they give the word, you guys foam the heck out of the house and get out. The Forest Service is directing all the units to go back out to the highway and stage there."

I looked over to the house, which was about two hundred yards behind the station. It was a new house that was nearing completion and it had several piles of construction debris around it. It sat in a clearing, and was far more defensible than the house on Danish Hollow Road.

Bob started the old fire truck and we drove over to the home. We pulled up along the side of the dwelling and went out to assess the place. The forest was about seventy-five feet away from the house on the south side. The owner had set up several sprinklers at the forests edge and they were soaking the trees and scrub. The inside of the house was nearly finished. It appeared that they were installing a wood floor when they were evacuated and, after that was completed, all that would be needed were appliances. I felt more confident that this home could be saved.

We pulled the hose line off the bed on the top of the engine and checked it to be sure we would be able to reach all corners of the house. Bob inspected the foam-producing mechanism on the truck while I dragged the hose to all sides of the house. Not much more to do but wait.

The smoke column had, once again, begun to rise up into the sky. There was a large mound to our south named Turkey Hill, where smoke was rising up, becoming very prominent. Wind was moving the treetops around and I could tell that the general trend was from the south and blowing northward. This would bring the fire in our direction. We sat on the tail end of the engine, both of us feeling confidant that we would, at the very least, be able to give this place a chance to survive. It was really in Mother Nature's hands after that.

A white pick-up truck came rolling up to the house and a dark-haired woman got out. I think she was with the Pinedale Fire Auxiliary. "How are you guys doing?" she asked. "Here, I brought you some breakfast." She handed us two Styrofoam plates heaped with scrambled eggs, sausage patties and toast. There was even a package of jam. Handing us another sack containing two pints of orange juice and some apples, she asked, "Do you need anything else?"

"No ma'am, I don't think so," I replied. "This is great just getting this meal. We we're thinking that we had been forgotten last night. Thank you so much." The woman told us that her son and daughter-in-law were building this house and hoped we would do all we could to save it for them. We reassured her that we would do everything within our power to do just that.

I mentioned to her that I could use some lip balm. My lips were beginning to get chapped to the point of being painful. I remembered reading somewhere that skiers, if finding themselves with no alternative, would rub their finger in the oils on top of their nose and apply that to their lips. I tried that, but it wasn't working for me. She said she would see what she could do and returned a few minutes later with a tube of balm. I don't think she realized how grateful I was for this. I would carry that lip balm with me for the duration of the fire.

As we sat down and dug into the meal she had brought out to us, I heard the far off drone of an airplane. It was getting louder and louder, until finally, it came over the valley where we sat. It was a spotter plane. That meant that an aerial assault would be underway soon. Spotter planes are used in advance of the big air tankers that drop the cranberry colored fire retardant. They fly into the area that is to be treated and visually spot the head of the fire. After deciding on the best approach, the big tanker follows the smaller spotter plane into the fire line. It was going on 10:30 a.m. and I was wondering what took them so long to get in the air. There were also helicopters flying into the Pinedale area but I couldn't see any water buckets dangling from them. "If this is an air assault, they had better start hitting it," I thought.

Bob and I sat and talked for another hour, never seeing the anticipated air tanker. We began hearing chatter over the radio. All of the various departments that were on scene had switched to the radio frequency known locally as Rim-Fire. It allowed for inter-agency communication. As the chatter increased, I began to watch the plume of smoke, which was starting to lean, buckling under the weight of itself. It was beginning to take on a more ominous color, changing from a dark gray to black and gray. I was getting uneasy and began scanning the rooftops of the homes on the hillside. On one of the roofs, I could see four or five men, binoculars in hand, scanning the mountain to our left.

"I think we're going to get the signal pretty damn soon," Bob said. I looked up to the top of Turkey Hill and could see the smoke actually moving now. Before, from a distance, the smoke seemed stationary, similar to watching clouds overhead. You know they are moving, but at an almost imperceptible speed.

All of a sudden, our radios began to shout, "Go, go, go." I looked up. The smoke had changed to a roiling mix of black, orange and yellow. Bob ran to the control panel of the engine. I jumped off of the bumper, nearly falling on my face, and ran to grab the nozzle.

"Charge the line, Bob," I shouted. He said something but I couldn't hear him over the roar of the engine. As he idled it up to charge the hose, he gave me a "thumbs up" sign and I could feel the line beginning to fill with water. I opened the nozzle and waited a moment for the foam to begin flowing. When it did, I started moving the stream back and forth, trying as best as I could to cover every square foot of the house with the sudsy mix. The foam was sticking to the walls and the roof of the house, telling me that the proportion of water to foam mixture was correct. I sprayed under the eaves of the home and anyplace where I thought an ember could land and possibly ignite.

I kept glancing up at the hill. Flames, some over a hundred feet high, could be seen racing through the trees at the top of the rise. I stepped up my pace, running around the perimeter of the house, spraying foam as I went. I didn't want to leave any surface untouched. This could be the only thing between the fire and the house that would protect it. The only thing between the homeowner's dreams and destruction.

When I was satisfied that the structure had been appropriately foamed, Bob shut down the line and I started dragging the hose back towards the engine. I left the nozzle wide open and began hoisting the hose over my shoulder in order to drain the water and foam from it. Bob was laying the hose in a back and forth pattern on the bumper of Engine 2 and then securing it with bungee cords. We wouldn't have time to do a proper hose-lay on the top of the engine.

With the lines secured, we jumped into the cab and began pulling out of the meadow. As we approached the blacktop and headed towards Highway 260, I could see that most of the fire vehicles were following suit. A line of red and lime-green fire trucks snaked their way out to a wide field at the intersection of Pinedale Rd. and Highway 260 to await further instructions.

Bob pulled Engine 2 onto to the highway and parked on the shoulder. We got out and looked back toward Pinedale, Turkey Hill and the fire, which was about to make an indelible mark on the picturesque little town. Huge, bright orange flames spewed over the top of the hill. The column of smoke, so visible for two days, had been replaced with a scene out of hell. The red barn, where the horse was housed, was empty. I didn't know if the old mare had been rescued or had simply gone inside out of fear, but it was too late to help her now.

Looking back at the covered bridge, I wondered if this would be the last time I would ever lay eyes on it.

Several engines began pulling out of the field and were turning east on Highway 260. As we hopped back into the cab thinking we would be given some different orders, the cell phone in the truck began to ring. I picked it up and it was Carol. "Are you OK?" she asked. "We've been watching the updates on TV and I was worried about you."

"I'm OK Carol." I was going to tell her about the evening in Pinedale but the phone, all of a sudden, had a rapid busy signal. Oh well. I was surprised she had not only been able to get through to me on the cell, but had been able to get hold of me in Pinedale. There is usually no cell phone signal out here because the nearest tower is in Show Low. I will try to call her when we get back to the Linden station, I thought. The landlines might be less busy than the cell phone circuitry.

A green Forest Service truck pulled up behind Engine 2 and a thin young man approached the cab. "We're going to have everyone stage just below Juniper Ridge," he told us. "We have the turnoff flagged with pink survey tape. There's a couple of guys waiting there for everyone and they'll tell you where to park." He turned and went back to his truck and drove over to another fire truck on the other side of the highway.

"Juniper Ridge?" Bob exclaimed. "Why, hell, that's five miles down the road. What do they think we can do out there?"

"Beats me," I replied. "I guess we should head over there and find out."

Bob pulled the engine out onto the roadway and we started toward the staging area. I could see a line of fire apparatus forming behind us, all going in the same direction.

The staging area was a large meadow on the north side of Highway 260. A man in a Forest Service uniform was waving the trucks down a bumpy dirt road and out into the middle of the field. Bob drove the engine to where he was pointing, dust kicking up in a brown cloud behind us. We were toward the western end of the meadow and other trucks were following us in and parking alongside. I could see vehicles from all over the state here. There was Tucson Fire, Golder Ranch Fire. Globe Fire, Phoenix Fire, Corona de Tucson Fire and many, many more.

"Someone has called out the Cavalry, Bob," I said, "look at all the different departments that are here."

"Yeah, I see them," Bob replied. "I don't like this too much. I just have a bad feeling about this whole thing." Bob lived in Timberland Acres and I knew he was worried about his home. I didn't really know what to say to him. I could've said, "hey, it'll be all right", but we had just witnessed how this fire had come up over Turkey Hill. I didn't want to be patronizing, so I just let it go. He had every right to be concerned about this monstrous blaze.

We jumped out of the cab and looked about. Engine 3 and two of our brush trucks were parked just down the line from us and we walked over to hang out with them. Almost everyone from the Linden department had climbed up on top of the hose beds. There was a better view from there and it also gave you a chance to stretch your legs out a bit. The talk was pretty much the same. How are we going to fight this fire from here? Where in hell are the airplanes? What is going on? They ought to be hitting this sucker hard!

I climbed up onto the hood of Engine 3 and sipped a Gator-Aide. It was hot out in this field and the dust was thick.

The Gator-Aide was warm, but it washed the grit from my throat.

Someone had handed out a box of MRE's (Meals Ready to Eat) to the crew of Brush 702 and they were passing them around to the Linden firefighters. I read the labels and they sounded practically gourmet. There were beef tips with noodles, lasagna, and one that everybody cautioned me about, chicken and dumplings. I took two boxes of the beef tips and stashed them under the seat of Engine 2, the memories of the bologna sandwiches and the cold Jack-in-the-Box hamburgers fresh in my mind. These would probably not be much better, but they couldn't be a heck of a lot worse.

I surveyed the scene that lay in front of me. There were over a hundred pieces of fire fighting equipment here in addition to a bulldozer on a flatbed trailer on the eastern side of the meadow. We were all just sitting here, hundreds of firefighters milling about in groups. A feeling of unease hung in the air. We felt like we were shirking our duty. The fire was in Pinedale. Right now. Why were they having us sit out in this meadow while Pinedale was burning? Is the Forest Service planning on fighting this fire at all? Those questions were on everyone's mind.

Chapter 12

I heard a loud droning sound and looked behind me to see a spotter plane and an air tanker flying in low, over the treetops. "It's about damned time," I thought. The fire had *obviously* moved into the town and huge, billowing clouds of smoke were rising high into the air. I say "obviously" because the smoke had changed. An occasional, low thudding noise signaled the demise of a propane tank, the explosion sending up a mushroom shaped cloud. When a structure would become engulfed, the smoke would turn a black, tar-like color for a brief time.

The air tanker disappeared into the smoke, approaching from the north, only to become visible again on the southeastern side of the fire. It was hard to tell if the crew had dropped their load of retardant or were aborting the pass. A few minutes later, the droning noise could be heard again and once more a spotter plane could be seen, leading in an air tanker. From our position on the ground, it was impossible to tell if this was a different plane or the same one making another attempt to drop its load. If I had to guess, I would say that it's the same one because it would have had to have flown to Winslow, some fifty miles to the north, to be refilled with slurry. If the plane was, indeed, dropping its load on the fire's front, it was having a negligible effect. The fire was burning with a frightening ferocity.

Looking off to the west, I sat there watching, my jaw slack with a sense of awe. I had never seen anything like this in my life. You could actually see the forward progress of the fire as it raced northward, a huge wall of smoke and flame that covered the entire western horizon. The colors from the conflagration were varied: yellow, mixed with orange, black and gray. The sun was, at times, completely obscured, and at other times an orange ball in the sky. From the way the fire was moving, it was evident that it was going to cross the highway, if it hadn't already. I looked around at the other firefighters and they were all staring at the wall of smoke and flames a few miles away. Some were becoming agitated at the thought of having to sit here, watching the fire burn into the town, and being able to do nothing. I heard the sound of several sirens approaching and looked up to see four vehicles from the Navajo County Sheriff's Office racing towards Pinedale.

"Now, what in hell do they think *they're* going to be able to do?" I asked Bob.

Bob chuckled and said, "I don't know. All the firefighters are sitting in this field."

In a near comedic skit, a few minutes later, the very same vehicles came racing back towards Show Low, lights flashing and sirens blaring. That bit of levity was a welcome respite to what we were witnessing.

I wondered how long we were going to be forced to sit in this meadow, and if whoever is in command of this fire is going to let us go in and try and save some of the town. Are we here as, merely, observers? I heard the sound of engines starting and saw three trucks begin to pull out towards the highway. They were the crews from Clay Springs, which is just a mile or so from Pinedale. "Finally," I thought, "We're going to do something."

They were the only vehicles to move and as they were leaving we could hear them on our radios, talking to each other. "Looks like we're on our own, guys," someone said. They pulled out onto Highway 260 and drove into the smoke and fire ahead of them. We knew what was happening. The

Pinedale-Clay Springs Fire Department personnel had broken ranks and were going in on their own to try and save their homes. The Forest Service and Navajo County Sheriff, Gary Butler, would later brand them "renegades" for their heroic attempt.

Somebody from the meadow answered the Clay Springs units. "You guys won't be on your own for long if we have anything to say about it." At this point, it didn't appear that we would be able to do anything but watch them go. The sight of them leaving and going out to do battle with this monster only inflamed the feelings of the rest of the firefighters. We knew how they felt. This is our mountain, communities and homes. The U.S.D.A. Forest Service was taking a different approach to fighting this fire. An approach that we weren't familiar with. An approach that was unacceptable to us. They were letting it burn.

A half an hour after Clay Springs had pulled out of the staging area, word began to spread that we were going to move. We thought that Pinedale would be the area that we would head to, possibly putting out any still-burning structures. We heard that, instead, all of the firefighters were being told by the Forest Service to go to the Show Low High School and stage there. We were incredulous. That's fifteen miles away from the fire. It was becoming obvious to us that the fire was going to be allowed to run through the pines and into the juniper and on into the grassland. The aerial attempt had been called off and all resources were being diverted into Show Low, which is the most populous town on the mountain. "No way," Bob told me. "They're not sending us into Show Low. This is our fire district. We're going back to the station."

We pulled into the parking lot of the Linden Fire Department and got out of the truck. The rest of the Linden crews, who had been out in the staging area, soon followed and parked their vehicles next to Engine 2. We stood in the parking lot and watched, as fire trucks from the Forest Service, and all over Arizona, made their way down Highway 260 and towards Show Low. We could not fathom why they had been sent that way. The fire is out here, in *our* area. The fire was spreading and beginning to threaten Linden. It was still in the Pinedale-Clay Springs fire district, but it was a short jump to Linden and Timberland Acres from there.

The mood amongst the Linden firefighters was not good. We had seen with our own eyes what had been allowed to occur in Pinedale. The fire came in and all resources were pulled out. The fire jumped the highway and all resources were sent to Show Low. There was a pattern beginning to take shape here. It was as if there was no plan in place at all. Or, the plan that *was* in place called for simply letting the fire have its own way, staying out of its path, and putting it out when it became a grass fire. *That* plan could include the loss of hundreds, if not thousands, of homes.

I looked out towards the west. The immense cloud of smoke showed no sign of subsiding. The firefighting equipment and personnel continued their move into Show Low, which is in the opposite direction of the fire. The Linden crew walked into the main station, one by one, feeling that we had deserted our neighbors in Clay Springs. We knew that a few miles to the west of us, they were doing what they could with three fire trucks and a handful of personnel, to save their homes. It wasn't right. We should be assisting them in any way we could.

I walked through the front door of the firehouse. Someone had brought in several boxes of pizza and they were strewn across the tables. I grabbed two slices and sat down to eat. The TV was on showing a news bulletin regarding the fire. I learned that the fire had been named the "Rodeo," due to the proximity of the rodeo grounds and the point of ignition. The reporter also said that a Type I team from Boise, Idaho had been assigned to try and quell the inferno. Larry Humphrey had been named the Incident Commander and Roy Hall, the Operations Commander. I recognized those names from somewhere, but could not put my finger on it. Oh well. Having a Type I team assigned to this fire meant that federal resources could be brought to bear on this fire, which was now well over 70,000 acres, and showing no sign of being tamed.

Chapter 13

Because we had been "grounded," there was not much to do but sit and wait. Chief Price advised us that the Sheriff's deputies would be stopping any private vehicles seen in the evacuation area. They were apparently concerned that there may be some looting in the now vacant neighborhoods. I wanted to go home and get some clean clothes and a quick nap and decided that, since I lived only a half-mile from the station, I would take a back road into my neighborhood.

I pulled into my driveway, got out and unlocked my front door. The first thing I noticed was the smell. There was no smoky odor. I remembered that I had left the air-conditioner on and was thankful that I had done so. This was the first clean air that I had breathed in three days. Man, did it taste sweet! I went into the bedroom and peeled off the orange Nomex coveralls and put on some clean jeans and a clean Linden Fire T-shirt. I went into our den and typed out an e-mail message, sending it to everyone in the address book, to let them know we were OK. Then I sat on the couch and leaned back onto my favorite piece of furniture.

My head had no sooner hit the pillow than there was a knock at my front door. I swung my feet off of the couch and went to the door. There stood a Sheriff's deputy with a piece of paper in his hand. He appeared to be Apache, but his badge said Navajo County Sheriff's Office. I opened the door. "How are you doing?" I greeted him.

He looked at me and said, "The fire's coming. You need to get out of here."

I'm sure he could see the Linden Fire insignia on my shirt. "Yeah, I know," I told him, "I just got back from

Pinedale. I came home for a few minutes and then I'm going back to the fire station."

"Well," he said, "You're going to have to sign this waiver stating that I made contact with you and told you to leave. I can't force you to go, but this will relieve the county of any liability if you get hurt."

"Partner," I said, "If I get hurt, it's not going to be because of anything the county did. It's going to be because of that big fire back there." I thought I saw a brief smile cross his lips, and I signed the waiver. Perhaps this would keep the deputies from beating on my door if I were able to come home later.

I lay back on the couch and closed my eyes. I don't know if it was from exhaustion or the countless cups of coffee I had drank, but my eyes seemed to flutter and not want to stay closed. I began hearing chatter on my radio and recognized the voices as some of my fellow Linden Fire personnel. They were in Pinedale and on their way to Clay Springs. Damn! They had somehow gotten through the gauntlet of Forest Service officials and were heading out to help the Pinedale-Clay Springs Department. I could hear Dewayne Saxton, Ryan Turner and Tim Dickinson, for sure. I thought I heard Tim Heims' voice, too. From what I could gather by the radio chatter, they were near the LDS church, which is a sort of mid-way point between Pinedale and Clay Springs. I could hear someone shouting, "Watch it, watch it," and it became obvious to me that they were in an area where the fire was getting ready to cross the highway. Again.

I got off of the couch, put the orange coveralls back on and locked the house up. I jumped into my Isuzu Trooper and headed back to the station. I doubted that I would be able to get out there, but if something happened and they needed more help, I would try to go. I could hear that they were triaging several homes in the Clay Springs area. Someone was calling for a chainsaw, while others were calling for foam. I heard someone from Clay Springs say, "Thanks, you guys. You don't know how much we appreciate this." The response came from Dewayne. "No problem. You guys would do it if it were us."

When I got back to the station it was clear that no one else would be allowed to go to the Clay Springs area. The Chief wanted to have, at least, some personnel in our district. Chief Price and some of the Sheriff's Department officials had been trying to work out a placard system that would allow the fire department personnel to travel in our district without fear of being pulled over. They decided that a white, 8x11, cardboard placard, with the Linden Fire logo printed on it would suffice. They were printed up and distributed to the personnel at the station. These were to be placed on the dashboard of the personal vehicles, thus, identifying them as members of the Linden Fire Department. For a reason that is still unknown, an hour later, this plan was scrapped. It was decided that the placards should, instead, be orange. Well, there was no orange cardboard to be had at the station and someone was going to have to go into Show Low to find some. I volunteered to go since I was unable to go to Clay Springs. Assistant Chief Ken Bantrum and I took our support vehicle (which is a pick-up truck that had been donated to the department and painted fire engine red) into town. The truck needed to be fueled and we could look for the orange paper while we were there.

When we got to the Show Low city limits, there was a roadblock set up. There were DPS, Show Low Police and Navajo County Sheriff's deputies manning it. All were heavily armed. They waved us through because we were in a marked fire department vehicle. As we went through the roadblock, I spotted a family on the side of the road. They had decorated several trees with red, white and blue ribbons and were waving at us. We waved back and drove on into Show Low. After gassing up the truck, we headed to the local K-Mart. We purchased several packages of multi-colored paper (which contained the orange color) and headed back to Linden. Again, we were waved through the roadblock. The family on the side of the road was still there and held up handmade signs that read, "Our Heroes." I hoped we could prove them right.

We arrived at the station, orange cardboard in hand. We took the paper upstairs to Carol Lewis, the Linden Fire Department Administrative Assistant. She was doing her level best to see that all requests were being met and trying to keep the many different agencies, that were growing hourly, on the same page.

It was now around 3:00 p.m. on Thursday, June 20th. The days were becoming a bit of a blur to me. I didn't know if it was from lack of sleep or the surreal atmosphere in which we now found ourselves. This was something that no one on this mountain, or in the State, for that matter, had faced before. I went back downstairs. I wanted another cup of coffee because it seemed to be what was sustaining me, keeping me going. Once there, I saw that there was another bulletin on the TV and I could not believe what I was hearing.

There is another fire. This one is due south of Heber-Overgaard. This can't be happening! There was a video showing a Phoenix news helicopter landing and picking up an obviously distraught young woman. She was holding a blanket or towel of some sort, and someone was leading her up to the chopper. I watched as they loaded her onto the craft and lifted off, the rotor wash from the chopper blades spreading coals and ash about the area. The reporter was calling her a lost "hiker" who had set a signal fire upon seeing the helicopter, which was in route that morning to cover the Rodeo Fire. *This* fire was already at two thousand acres and burning out of control near an area known as Chediski Peak. I looked at the Forest Service map, which had been taped to a chalkboard in the meeting room, and saw that the location of the fire would put the community of Heber-Overgaard directly in its sights, if it were not brought under control.

I walked to the parking lot and looked out on the western skyline. Even though the smoke from the inferno in Pinedale and Clay Springs was very much visible, a new column of smoke was taking shape. The color of this new tower was slightly more gray and appeared to be further away, the entire top of the column being visible. It reminded me of the view I had from the Show Low airport two days ago, when the Rodeo Fire was still in its infancy.

At that particular moment, I felt as though every last bit of energy in my body was draining out through my feet. All I could do was to stand and stare at this vision that was before me. The small community of Linden, Arizona looked, quite literally, like a war zone. Great plumes of smoke, as far as the eye could see, now scarred the view normally afforded, one of thick pine forests and rolling, grassy meadows. A sickly orange pall, and a light that cast blue shadows on the ground, had replaced the usually bright, yellow sunshine.

In a twisted bit of fire logic, I felt a raindrop. The fire in the Pinedale area was burning so hot that it had created a pyro-cummulous cloud over itself, wrenching every last bit of humidity from the air and sending it up in a fake thunderhead. I looked around to see if someone else was feeling the rain. It was so brief, and the drops so small, that I thought for a moment that I was imagining it. The rain, however, was leaving marks on the concrete. They were spaced at a drop per square foot, but it was real. It was another example of the topsy-turvy situation in which we find ourselves. The lack of rain is a main contributor to the fire, and now, the fire itself, is making rain.

Chapter 14

The crews that had been helping out in Clay Springs began to return to the station. I had been busy helping out around the firehouse. Linden Fire Department was going to be the command post for fire operations due to the proximity to the fire and much needed to be done. Cots were being placed in the west bay for the firefighters who were here from other districts and the Salvation Army was setting up a mobile kitchen to help feed the crews. Large box trucks were beginning to show up at the department, loaded with bread and buns and water. I helped unload and stack the food that was being brought in.

There were the Sheriff's Auxiliary folks who had been mobilized and were asking nearly everyone if they needed anything. In a politically incorrect (but welcome) move, they brought in a pick-up truck loaded with tobacco products. There was chewing tobacco and a variety of cigarettes. It may seem ironic, but after breathing the dense, harsh smoke from a forest fire, tobacco was actually a "sweet smoke," offering a welcome break.

That's something I've always admired about the people on this mountain. They live their life in real time. If the boys on the fire line need smokes, well then, by God, they're going to get them. Another commodity that began showing up in abundance was toilet paper. Known as "mountain money" to the seasoned wildland firefighters, it is a little thought of, but sorely missed item.

The guys that had returned from Pinedale seemed to be pleased with what progress they had been able to achieve. Several vulnerable homes had been triaged, that is, trees and brush close to the house had been removed and the entire structure foamed. The look on their faces when learning of the new fire, was taking some of the shine from their earlier accomplishments.

Evening was beginning to settle in and the fire was starting to show signs of lying down, but there was still an orange glow behind Juniper Ridge. I walked into the west bay and saw that, already, there were firefighters who had found the cots and were trying to get some sleep. For some reason, electricity to the firehouse and the surrounding area had been cut. A diesel generator had been brought in to supply power to the station and there was a continuous whine from the motor. That didn't seem to be bothering the firefighters on the cots, as this was the first sleep many of them had had for two days.

I decided that, since there was nothing else we could do until morning, I would go home and get my small generator connected to our freezer. I didn't know if I would be able to keep it running long enough to save the meats and other frozen items, but I was going to try. I was amazed to find that my neighborhood, though less than a mile away, still had power.

Ash was beginning to fall from the sky once again and, since I didn't have to worry about the generator, I decided to try and wet down the roof of our house. I turned on the hose and discovered that our water pressure, which was normally very high, was reduced to a trickle. Driving down the road on my way home, I noticed that one of my neighbors had set a water sprinkler on his roof, hoping that this would be sufficient to ward off the fire that was steadily advancing toward Linden. Because I was at the end of the water line, this was probably what was further reducing the water pressure.

I did what I could with the little pressure I had, putting my thumb over the end of the hose and spraying a meager mist over the roof. It was evaporating within minutes, so I turned my attention to watering the maple trees I had planted a few weeks earlier. The beautiful Sunset Maple in my front yard was wilted badly. I rubbed one its leaves between my fingers and it felt like paper. It had become another victim of the drought. I had been watering it every other day, but it had gone for three days without water and was unable to tolerate the lack of moisture. I watered it anyway, hoping for the best.

It was well after dark now, and the smoke was starting to get very thick outside. I wanted a shower and decided that I would try to take one, even with the low water pressure. I practically had to dance around in the shower stall to get wet, but it was invigorating to finally be able to wash the stench of the fire off of myself. I looked at the water going down the drain and it was the color of soot.

After drying off and putting on some sweatpants, I went to the kitchen and poured three fingers of whiskey over ice and added a splash of water. I hoped that this would override all of the caffeine I had been ingesting, and allow me to get some sleep. It was working. I could feel the warm glow of the alcohol taking effect and at 10:30 p.m. crawled into my bed and closed my eyes.

It seems as though I had just shut my eyes when my radio started crackling, waking me up. I looked at the clock on the nightstand. It was 11:30 p.m. I recognized the voice on the radio. It was Bob Filley. He had gone home to get some rest also, but that wasn't going to happen tonight. "Ok," he said, "the fire has just come up over Juniper Ridge."

I lay there for a moment, knowing I would have to get up and go back to the station. The few moments of sleep that I had gotten only exacerbated the fatigue and weariness. The fire was now over the ridge and I knew what that meant.

Timberland Acres was going to be the next target for this
blaze. I didn't know what we were going to be able to do. It
was near midnight and pitch black outside but I had to go back
to the station to see what, if any, plans were in the works. My
radio began to chatter again. It was Chief Price. "I want all
personnel to return to the station. Repeat. All personnel to the
station."

I swung my feet over the edge of the bed and rubbed
my eyes. They felt swollen and gritty from lack of sleep. As I
sat there, waking up, the phone rang. It was Troy Hvidsten.
Troy was one of three full timers on the Linden Fire
Department. "Umm, yeah Gary. Are you coming down here?"
he asked.

"I'll be there in a few minutes," I replied, "I'm just
getting dressed."

I put on my jeans and a T-shirt and struggled to get into
my boots. After putting the orange jumpsuit back on, I
grabbed a cap and headed out the door.

Walking outside, the stench of smoke hit me like a wall.
It nearly made me nauseous. The brief respite from the smoke
inside my air-conditioned house had been most welcome, but I
knew that within a few minutes I would hardly notice the acrid
odor. I jumped in my truck and drove towards the highway.
Juniper Ridge was directly in front of me as I drove to the
station. It was about five miles to the west and I could see
orange fingers of flame. It was definitely over the top of the
ridge and burning into some of the juniper and grasses that
lined the hill. The nearest home was only a quarter of a mile
away.

Pulling into the parking lot at the station, I could see
that nearly everyone was here. Dewayne pulled in right behind
me and we walked into the meeting room together. Assistant

Chief Eddie Morin was having an animated conversation with several of the firefighters, most of whom had homes in Timberland Acres. He had apparently driven out to T/A to get an assessment of the situation and was relaying what he saw. "It's laying down right now. The flames are only about a foot tall," he said, "and I think we can keep it from running up into the area."

He drew a diagram on the chalkboard, highlighting where the fire was and where he thought it was going to go. I looked around the room. There were a few guys from Linden-Pierce Construction here. They had been enlisted as water tender drivers and bulldozer operators, two very vital keys to firefighting operations. C.D. Nunally, Ryan Turner and Bob Filley, all of whom have homes in T/A, were huddled around Eddie Morin, listening intently to a plan being hatched to stop the fire from running up into the houses that lay a few hundred yards away.

The plan called for taking several water tenders and a bulldozer up to the road above the fire. Once there, the dozer would start pushing dirt down the hill towards the fire, depriving it of any combustible material, and the water tenders were to soak the sides of the roadway. The fire would have no choice but to run in a different direction away from the houses.

After assigning the different pieces of apparatus, a crew of men headed towards Timberland Acres to engage the fire before it had a chance to get up and run. The vehicles drove down Timberland Road. When they came to the intersection with Deer Run Road, a man in a Forest Service truck tried to flag the vehicles down. They knew that he would attempt to prevent them from going any further so they drove past him and continued on to the top of the hill. Once there, each person did as they had been told. While the dozer went to work on the hill above the fire, the water tenders began soaking the sides of the roadway. The tenders drove through the area in a loop, stopping at the Linden sub-station to refill with water, when needed. The dozer knocked down some small trees that lined the road, and began pushing dirt into the fires path.

Because all of the equipment had been assigned, I had to wait at the main station as a backup driver, should one be needed. Several cots had been brought into the room and anyone who was not in T/A was trying to rest. The cots, although they allowed you to stretch out, were less than comfortable. The nylon covering was incredibly taut and I jokingly said to someone that you could probably bounce a quarter ten feet in the air off of it. I lay there, trying to sleep, awaiting the call for a new driver.

Shortly before daylight, the crew from Timberland Acres arrived back at the main station, after having been discovered by some people from the Forest Service while carrying out the clandestine operation. Under threat of arrest, they had been advised to leave the area, being told that Forest Service crews would take up where they were leaving off at daybreak. Forest Service, technically, had command of the area and the Linden Fire crews begrudgingly left the area, hoping that the government crews would be true to their word. We were less than hopeful, having seen how the fire had been managed to this point.

Most of the guys thought that what they had been able to do out there would save some homes, but were disappointed that the Forest Service crews hadn't immediately begun to take over. Their big, wide blade bulldozer could have done in minutes what would've taken hours for the smaller, privately owned dozer to do. We would later learn that the Forest Service bulldozer was never even taken off of the trailer.

Chapter 15

When the fire breached Juniper Ridge it became obvious that there would be further evacuations. At the rate that this fire had been burning, failure to contain it in Timberland Acres would leave it a few short miles from Show Low. As it began to get light outside, more police and fire officials were arriving at the department. I went outside and called Carol on her cell phone.

After spending the previous night at the house in White Mountain Lake, Steve decided that they should stay at his house in Show Low. Unlike the other home, he had an evaporative cooler there and it would be much more comfortable. Besides, there had been no evacuation order given as of yet. I knew that was about to change. It was unclear when the order would be given, but Show Low was going to be evacuated and I wanted them to be on their toes when that happened. I told her to be prepared and get out of there as soon as she could. This was early morning and most people were still in bed, so I doubted that the order was going to be given immediately. More likely, the police would wait until mid-morning to announce the evacuation so that people would be awake and the exodus would, perhaps, be more orderly.

Up to this point, the local fire agencies were not fully aware of the scope of this fire. We were going on what we could glean from newscasts, which were now national as well as local, and, what we could learn from the Forest Service. We knew that it was a huge fire, starting in Cibecue and now knocking on our own front door, but that was about it. It was being reported that the newly named "Chediski Fire" was approaching 70,000 acres and still burning out of control.

Heber-Overgaard was going to be evacuated, and the residents there would be sent to Payson or Holbrook. It is beginning to appear as though this whole mountain is going to burn and no one can do a damned thing about it.

One of the people to arrive at the firehouse was a tall, lanky man, whom I guessed to be in his early forties, named Don Howard. He was with Summit Fire, out of Flagstaff, and specialized in structure protection. With his arrival, our period of being in the dark over this fire was about to end. I could tell that he was highly respected among the different department heads, now at the Linden Fire Department, but Don seemed to be genuinely concerned about how the firefighters themselves were dealing with this inferno.

He walked over to the chalkboard, which still had the diagram mapping out last nights attempt to head off the fire in Timberland Acres, and put up a map of the area that the fire had already burned. There were two distinct features on this map, the largest being the area that the Rodeo fire had consumed, which was now well over 100,000 acres. The other area was the Chediski fire and it showed a large, finger-like burn pattern that was leaning in towards the Rodeo fire. The firefighters in the room began huddling around this map, as it was the first aerial assessment we had seen. So this was the beast we were up against. Not one, but two separate fires, both having the potential to be catastrophic.

Don asked the firefighters in the room to settle down and listen up. He introduced himself and said he wanted to do a morning briefing on the progress of the fire and what resources would be coming into our area. With the map to his back, he said that it was very likely, if not certain, that the Chediski Fire and the Rodeo Fire, would merge, forming a fire complex never seen in the state of Arizona. Already, he explained, veteran firefighters from around the country were seeing fire behavior never before observed, anywhere. The conditions that brought us to this point had been unmatched in the annals of firefighting history. The record drought, which has left live trees with an interior moisture content of less than that of kiln-dried lumber, the bark beetle infestation, and the wildland-urban interface had formed an unholy triad that was now manifesting itself in the guise of this fire. We cannot fight this fire head-on, he said, but it can be fought with back burns and fire lines. We can do what we can to triage the homes in its path, but some homes were going to be lost. An area of particular interest, he said, was Hop Canyon. This is on the Apache Reservation and was being used as the trigger point for evacuating Show Low. If the fire reached this point, the evacuation order would be given. He concluded the morning briefing at this point and went upstairs to speak with the other officials.

Several firefighters had stepped outside and were smoking cigarettes and drinking coffee while talking amongst themselves and looking off to the western horizon. It was now around 9:00 a.m. and the fire was starting to get legs. Large columns of smoke were already forming over Juniper Ridge and I felt awful for the people who owned homes in T/A. That area, just yesterday so green and serene, will never be the same after today. It's already been burned beyond recognition in some areas, and now, it's just a matter of time before the rest of the region will feel the impact from this duo of encroaching flames. Bob Filley, in particular, seemed to be resigned to the fact that he would lose his home. I remembered his words from the other night in Pinedale about how he "didn't like this one bit." I didn't argue with him then and I surely was not going to do so now. He had seen where the fire was coming over the ridge and could probably gauge where it would go. I wished that there was a way to comfort him, but everyone was concerned about their own homes.

I went back into the station and watched the newscast playing on the TV. There were now constant updates about the fire on all of the local channels as well as the national news programs. One particular gentleman, Jim Paxon, had been designated as the media spokesperson. He would relay information about the progress of the fire and what, if any, containment was being achieved. With his southwestern drawl, he would tell viewers in a no-nonsense way, that this fire was absolutely dangerous and, at this time, completely out of control. His media briefings were being held at the Show Low High School, which had been set up as a media encampment and a commissary.

From the view afforded by the cameras, I couldn't recognize this as the local high school. There were dozens of large vans, all with satellite dishes pointed to the sky, and large, circus type tents set up everywhere. Nearly every briefing was accompanied by camera shots of the omnipresent smoke columns rising high into the sky. It made for dramatic television, no doubt about it. Mr. Paxon was making mention of the Chediski Fire and reiterating the fact that evacuations were very likely to be occurring, sooner than later.

Stepping outside, I stood in the parking lot and once again, my gaze went to the smoke to our west. I checked my cell phone and saw a good signal so I called my dad to let him know that I was OK and to give him an idea of what was going on up here on the mountain.

My dad, Harold, and his wife Anna had lived in Pinetop for twenty-five years before relocating to Tucson. They, and my grandparents, lived on adjoining lots on the outskirts of

Pinetop. I understood their need to move back to Tucson. Medical and insurance needs were dictating that they had to be closer to a large city and, because Tucson had once been their home, they decided to move back.

It must have been hard for them to leave their mountain retreat, I think, no matter how much they would try to deny it. Their property had large oak and pine trees, along with apple and cherry trees. There was a peach tree that my stepsister had brought up from Tucson and planted and a maple tree that my grandmother, Helen, brought from Indiana and planted. Both trees were doing well and held fond memories for them. There was also a huge lilac bush in my grandfather's front yard that was transplanted from a settlers cabin in Linden. It was also doing very well and I even took some shoots from it back to Linden to be planted in my own yard. There were raccoon and gray squirrels as well as black bears and a variety of birds that were always present when I would visit. It seemed to me to be an enchanted place. A cool, quiet respite from the rigors of city life.

When my dad answered the phone I tried to give him an overview of what was taking place. I told him that Carol and the cats were safe, but Show Low and the surrounding communities were going to be evacuated soon. The fire was still out of control and it was *in* Linden, but still several miles from our house. He told me to be careful and before I hung up the phone, I did something that I had rarely done in the past. I told my father that I loved him.

Chapter 16

At approximately 3:00 p.m. there was a commotion from the Chiefs' office upstairs. An order had been given for the city of Show Low to be on stand-by for evacuation. This time, if an evacuation order were to be put into effect, it would be a major undertaking. With the communities of not only Show Low, but also Pinetop-Lakeside and the Reservation towns of Hondah and McNary being evacuated, there would be a relocation of over 30,000 people. The evacuees, like the ones before, would be told to go to the Round Valley Gymnasium in Springerville. The people being relocated in Hondah and McNary would be directed to go to Whiteriver.

I called Carol as soon as I heard of the stand-by order to evacuate and told her to get moving. Again, she would have a slight head start on the traffic, which was sure to be heavy, very soon. She and Steve's fiancée, Cindy, left immediately while Steve lingered behind to load some personal items before he left. I was glad that I had been able to get through to her because I knew that the phone lines were sure to be jammed in a short while.

Carol told me that she had been in touch with the company that we did our contract courier business with, and they were being very understanding about the plight of our communities. Most of the medical offices were being closed and the ones that remained open would have to have their lab specimens rerouted through Flagstaff. As far as my route was concerned, Cibecue was shut down and another courier company had stepped in to move the specimens from the Whiteriver Hospital to Phoenix in the interim. I knew that it was simply a matter of time before the major highways to Phoenix would be completely closed, and I was grateful for the other company's assistance, even if they were considered "the competition." It was heartwarming to see how people would pitch in to help each other when it became necessary to do so.

At around 5:00 p.m. the order to evacuate was given. With the evacuation in full swing, the media were in a frenzy trying to get pictures of the lines of cars leaving Show Low. This was national news now, and all of the major networks were breaking in to their regularly scheduled programming to bring the latest shots of the exodus. To me, it was heartbreaking. This had to be bringing home to the residents on the mountain the very real possibility that there may not be a town left here when they return. There was a feeling in the air of impending catastrophe and yet, there was still a sense of hope.

Most of these people had seen wildfires before. The sight of a smoke column on the horizon had become an all too familiar sight in recent years. Sometimes the columns were from burns being conducted by the Forest Service or the White Mountain Apache Tribe and at other times, there were true wild fires on the loose. Usually, these smoke columns would be off in the distance and too far away to be of concern. There were also times when the citizens of the mountain would complain vehemently about the smoke that would settle into the valleys and neighborhoods during prescribed burns. As recently as two years ago, a burn had been halted due the vociferous folks that had attended a city council meeting.

I wondered how these people must be feeling now. Was it possible that the prescribed burn that they were complaining about would be the one area to be spared the fire's wrath? Oh well. There is no use in trying to second-guess anything now. There will be misery to spare before this is all over.

Earlier in the day, before the evacuation started, we had watched the smoke rising over Juniper Ridge. Several other columns could be seen forming to the southeast. They were turning an ugly black color. Don Howard walked out into the parking lot and saw that there were several firefighters watching the curling towers. He told us that the smoke to the south was from an effort to burn out some of the fires fuel. The idea was to redirect the fire to an area that had been previously burned.

We could hear the drone of a spotter plane. I watched the plane skim the horizon to our south and bank off towards Timberland Acres. There was no tanker behind it and I assumed that it was doing an aerial reconnaissance. There has been a lingering question among most of the firefighters regarding the aerial attack on the fire. It seemed to us that the best time to hit the fire from the air would be early in the morning. The smoke would not have a chance to rise up and the flames would still be lying close to the ground. From what we have witnessed though, the air attacks have mostly begun at mid-afternoon.

As the day wore on, there began to be a number of fire engines entering the Linden area. Some of these engines had no emblems on them and I assumed they were either State or Federal firefighters coming in to help with structure protection. There were also crews being brought in from out of State and from out of the country, for that matter. I saw a crew walking into the east bay of the Linden Fire Department with insignias on their shirts identifying them as being from Puerto Rico.

The field on the west side of our department had been bulldozed flat and was now a staging area for the many brush trucks and engines that were arriving by the minute. A line of portable toilets had been set up in the same lot to accommodate the hundreds of firefighters now descending upon our once quiet, rural station.

The east bay of the department, our largest, was now being used to store the vast amount of supplies pouring into the area. The dry bologna sandwiches and cold Jack-in-the-Box hamburgers were mere memories now. Inside the bay were boxes of melons and fresh fruit, bottled water and Gator-Aide by the case full, sandwiches of all sorts and an assortment of sweets. The lot to the east of the station was home to Linden-Pierce Construction and it had been turned into combination parking lot and hay barn. There were hundreds of bales of hay being brought in for the livestock left behind in the evacuation and a crew was assigned to seek them out and drop off feed for them. There was not only hay for the livestock, but also dog food, cat food and poultry food as well. I was glad to see that the animals had not been forgotten and thoughts of the old gray cat and the chestnut-brown mare in Pinedale came back to me.

Among the many supplies being delivered was an assortment of personal hygiene products such as toothpaste, eye drops and toilet paper. I noticed that some of the Linden firefighters were wearing kerchiefs around their necks. They were decorated like the American flag with red, white and blue and the stars and stripes. I wanted one. It would not only come in handy for filtering the smoke from the air, but, because I saw only the Linden crew wearing them, would be a symbol of solidarity on our department. They were being handed out upstairs in the Chiefs' office and I immediately went to retrieve one. I folded the kerchief in a triangle and tied it around my neck. It would prove to be an invaluable piece of gear for keeping the harsh smoke from my lungs. There was also a box of leather gloves and each firefighter was getting a pair. They were more versatile than the bulky firefighting gloves in our turnout gear and would save our hands from splinters and minor burns.

Going back downstairs, I saw that there were a number of tables and chairs being set up as a makeshift cafeteria. I helped set them up and began looking for other ways to help out. One of our firefighters, Art Johnson, was loading up the rescue truck with bags of dog, cat and poultry feed and I went over to help him. He was part of a crew assigned to scour the neighborhoods in Linden and feed any animals they came across. I helped him throw some bags of feed onto the truck. After checking his load to be sure that he had a good variety, he left to go in search of hungry animals.

I knew that he would not be going into Timberland Acres. There was no way to know what manner of hell could be happening in there right now. The smoke from the fire was visible in four separate columns now. Two of the columns were from burnout operations and the other two were the heads of the Chediski and the Rodeo fires. When it was safe, we would send a crew in to see what damage had been done, but right now the fire was burning too hot to even consider that. Perhaps, after dark, the fire will lie down again and we will be able to get someone in there.

Tim Heim approached me after Art had left. Someone had seen a couple of dogs in a pen in Cheney Ranch and the Chief wanted us to go out and check on them. Tim and I joined the department within days of each other and we had become good friends. Tim is an affable fellow who had, until recently, worked as a counselor at the American Indian Christian Mission, which is located in Linden. He currently works for the Forest Service and, like myself, is a volunteer

Linden firefighter. Standing at 6'5", his nickname is Tiny Tim. He had begun to shoulder some of the duties of being the local IC (Incident Commander) thus giving Chief Price a chance to rest and collect her thoughts. Tim and I loaded into Succor (our smallest brush truck) and drove out to check on the animals.

At the end of Dreamy Draw Rd. in Cheney Ranch, we found the two dogs we were looking for. They were in a chain-link pen, measuring 20x20, and had no food or water in their dishes. They were beautiful dogs, two Akitas that looked to have been well cared for. Apparently the people who owned the home, and the dogs, were in Phoenix and had been unable to get back home before the roads were closed. They called the fire department asking that someone check on the dogs. Tim and I put out food and water and then spent a few minutes romping around with them. It was obvious that they were lacking the attention normally given them by their owners, and they were in the mood to play.

After returning to the brush truck, we drove back down Dreamy Draw and stopped at the intersection with Cheney Ranch Loop. There is a house there that sits on the top of a hill and allows a panoramic view of the entire Linden valley. Tim, who is a respectable photographer, wanted to try and get some shots of the fire, which was still creeping around Juniper Ridge. We parked the truck and walked to the highest point on the property and looked out over the valley. The scene before us was unbelievable.

The sun was about thirty degrees above the western horizon and nearly obscured by the clouds of smoke rolling across its face. It was a deep orange color and the entire orb was visible. In the distance, a giant Sekorski helicopter floated across the sky. Looking like a huge, metal dragonfly, it had a large hose dangling from its middle. The chopper would hover over lakes or ponds and suck up water at a rate of three hundred gallons per minute and deliver it to wherever it needed to be dropped. Dense smoke hung in the air, and in the valley it was beginning to hug the ground like fog. It was a near apocalyptic vision and one that I hoped I would never have to witness again. After Tiny Tim shot a few pictures we got back in the truck and drove back to the station.

There were now live radio broadcasts being done by a reporter who, I assume, had binoculars and was reporting from some distance away from the fire. At one point, he told his audience that he could see homes burning in the Timberland Acres area. He would recant this, however, an hour or so later. So far, we had not heard of any homes being burned, but from the way the fire was moving in that region, it was obvious that some homes had to have been destroyed. Our worst fears for Timberland Acres had been realized. The fire was loose in the subdivision and burning with a ferocity that we could never have imagined.

Several attempts had been made to change the direction of the blaze, but they had been unsuccessful. An old ranch about a mile from the entrance to Timberland Acres was the focal point of these operations. The ranch had several pastures that could be utilized as fire breaks to try and keep the fire from crossing the highway and running into the north side of Linden. Bulldozers were brought into that area and had cut several wide lines to the south in an effort to keep the fire in the foothills of T/A. Further to the east, in Cheney Ranch, dozers and Forest Service crews were working to cut a fire line above the homes there, just in case the line at the old ranch house was breached. A back burn operation had been attempted also, but it was unknown to us at the department what sort of progress had been made.

The engines without emblems on them, I came to learn, *were* State Fire crews that had been brought in to do structure protection. They were in Cheney Ranch now, triaging as many homes as they could. There were crews from Linden, Show Low and several other departments from around the state doing the same thing. The homes that had a high likelihood of being saved would be foamed after having removed any trees or brush near the house. It was sure to make some people angry, upon returning home, to see that their landscape had been dramatically changed. This was assuming that they would have a home to return to. Homes that had been deemed unviable were flagged with a red ribbon, signifying that it would be too dangerous for the firefighters too try and save that house. I believe that there were more homes being red-flagged than green-flagged, the green flag labeling the home as being "defensible."

People have moved into this environment to live among the trees. The problem is, a lot of folks just don't want to cut down any trees at all. I have seen many homes on the mountain that have branches hanging on top of the roofs and against the walls. Should these trees ignite, there is simply nothing you can do to save the home. If you compound this situation a hundred fold, then you can get an idea of what these crews were up against.

The smoke from the back burn was starting to climb high into the sky. From my vantage point at the station, there appeared to be more than one operation going on, as there were four distinct columns that I could see. The fire still seemed to be quite a long way from Cheney Ranch. There was a crew still trying to doze a line above the homes there, so I knew that there was concern about the fire running over the hill and down into the subdivision. I could not fathom that happening. If the fire made it that far, then the rest of Linden would meet the same fate as Timberland Acres, with fire running unabated through the community. After having seen how the Forest Service has dealt with the fire every time it made a push into an inhabited area, I was feeling less than confident about how they would handle the situation with Cheney Ranch.

I walked into the meeting room inside the station. Chief Price was talking with Sid Howard from Pinedale-Clay Springs Fire and I heard her say something to the effect of, "Well, I guess I'll finally get that new, Grecian tub I've always wanted, Sid." After she had finished her conversation with Chief Howard, I asked her what she had meant about the "new tub." With a resigned tone to her voice she told me, "After tonight, I will probably not be able to go home again." She said that the head of the fire was expected to come into the rest of Linden this evening and her home would be directly in its path. She was making plans for a new home. One with a Grecian bathtub.

A dark, sinking feeling came over me. I simply did not want to believe that this was going to happen. I thought of the many times I had driven out on the 300 Road (or Rim Road, as it's also known) and looked out over the vast swaths of pine trees, as far as the eye could see. I remembered driving the road from Linden to Pinedale in the evening, just to see the deer and elk and fox. Most of this has already burned. It is gone. I thought about the Black Canyon road that runs behind Heber-Overgaard and comes back out onto Highway 260 near Clay Springs. There were several historic ruins back there, along with a trio of graves from some long ago feud between cowboys. This, in all likelihood, is gone also. Now, the fire is going to try and consume the place Carol and I had chosen to call our home.

Chapter 17

For the first time since this fire had started, a wave of true depression began to wash over me. I needed to talk to Carol. I called her on my cell phone, which was beginning to run low on power. I knew that she would be glad to hear from me, even though she was going through her own ordeal. When she answered the phone, I felt my dark mood lift a bit. I had to let her know that the fire was going to be here tonight. In what I think was the most difficult thing I've ever had to say to her, I told her, "We have to decide what we're going to do if our house burns down." I hated the fact that I had to say this, but she needed to understand the gravity of this situation. "I'm going to go get some things from the house. Are there any specific items you want? I'll get clothes for both of us, but are there any items we cannot live without?" I asked her.

How do you choose what things to throw to the fire? What mementos from your life do you willingly leave behind? We had saved our important documents, our cats and ourselves. But, how do you mentally sort through all of your belongings and decide what to leave behind? I could tell that she was becoming distraught over having to make this choice.

"I don't know, Honey," she replied. "Just get what you can."

I told Chief Price that I wanted to go home to retrieve some items and she said that I should take her car, as it was bigger than mine. I drove home and pulled the Chiefs' Suburban up to the front steps. Our house had never looked more perfect. During our day-to-day routine, we take advantage of the fact that our home will always be there, but now, faced with the likelihood of its destruction, I looked at my home in a different light. It looked absolutely perfect. It was the home in the woods that we had always wanted, and even though it was shrouded in smoke, it still looked beautiful.

Walking inside, I tried to decide what to get. Clothes would be the most important item, so I grabbed armfuls of Carols' clothes from her closet and threw them into the back of the Suburban. I was less choosy about my clothes and grabbed several pairs of jeans and some T-shirts along with a couple of long-sleeved shirts. I pulled an expensive Navajo sand painting from the wall and loaded that into the truck and next, decided to load my music collection. I had two cabinets full of cassette tapes that I knew could not be replaced. The cabinets were brand new, made of oak. I taped the doors closed and hoisted them up and out the door. Once *they* were loaded into the truck, it was full.

I drove back to the station to pack what I had just retrieved from the house, into my Trooper. As I was doing this, my phone rang and it was Carol. "Don't forget to get our photo albums," she told me. This stopped me in my tracks. Here I was, saving the things that were monetarily replaceable, but she had the common sense to remember the things that were *truly* irreplaceable. Our photo albums contained all the memories of our many years together and could never have been replaced. I thanked her for reminding me of what was really important. I went back home and picked up every photograph I could find.

When I got back to the station, it was becoming obvious that the fire would, indeed, make its run into our community tonight. Predictably, there was beginning to be a procession of firefighting equipment leaving the area. Smoke had begun to stretch across the southern horizon, now a swath of darkness, extending from T/A to directly in front of the firehouse. It was deemed too dangerous for the crews to stay in the path of the fire so they were, once again, being directed to Show Low. As evening began to fall, there were very few firefighters left in our district, except for the Linden Fire Department personnel. The Salvation Army mobile kitchen was packing up, after having fed hundreds of hungry firefighters throughout the day.

I walked into the meeting room and saw that there were a few people, not from our department, still here. There were three very large men sitting at a table with a pan of barbecued chicken left behind by the mobile kitchen. They were completely engrossed in finishing it off. I recognized them as a crew sent here from Kentucky. I could hear them talking amongst themselves about how, "Ain't no little fire gonna keep us from eatin' supper." I had to admire their bravado, because the fire was beginning to loom large across the highway. I don't know how they slipped away, but I wouldn't see them again.

In the parking lot, the officers on the department were trying to figure out what to do with our firefighting apparatus. It was decided that the safest place for the equipment to be was in a large cinder pit directly behind the firehouse. It was large enough to accommodate not only the fire trucks and water tenders, but also our personal vehicles. There was gravel for several hundred yards around the area and it would serve as an ideal firebreak.

While some of the firefighters were moving the vehicles, others began to remove some large juniper trees that lined the entrance to the fire department. They were unceremoniously cut down with chain saws and moved away from the driveway. After they were cut, the focus shifted to the other side of the highway. Some large pinion and juniper were likewise removed and a water tender began soaking the roadside in an effort to prevent the fire from running right up to the edge of the highway. Once this was done, all we could do was sit and watch as the fire made its run over the ridge.

It was starting to get dark now and the fire was making itself known in earnest. Looking to the southern horizon, the orange glow from the fire, which had not yet come over the top, stretched for nearly five miles. It was burning so hot that huge balls of flame were exploding over the top of the ridge, as unburned gasses became super-heated and ignited. The sight was at once beautiful and terrifying. I had never, in my life, witnessed anything like it.

The emotional toll this disaster was taking was starting to become evident. I looked over to Carol Lewis, who owns a home in Cheney Ranch, and she was sobbing as she gazed across the highway toward the oncoming inferno. A member of the Linden Fire Board and his son had been helping to fight the fire and now, as it was making its approach, the father demanded that the son leave Linden and go back to Show Low. I understood his concern. It's one thing to put yourself in the path of certain danger but another thing entirely to put your child there. The son reluctantly left Linden, obeying his father's wishes.

I could see that Garry Moore was becoming agitated. The fire, even though we could not yet see the actual flames, was getting brighter by the minute. He was debating whether or not he should leave to go and be with his wife, or stay, and have the fire, possibly, burn over the top of us.

He was not alone. I was wondering the very same thing. The sight of this monstrosity looming just the other side of the ridge was frightening, at the very least. It was all I could do to keep from going to the cinder pit, jumping in my truck and getting the hell out of there. I told Garry that we should go check on the vehicles behind the station, hoping that if we got the fire out of our vision it would calm us down.

We got about a hundred yards from the station and stopped. We could actually hear the fire now. So. The monster has a voice. It sounds like a low flying jet airplane and it is flying in our direction. This did little to ease the anxiety so we wheeled around and headed back up to the parking lot.

The Linden firefighters were huddled in groups, some taking photos and some just staring at the hellish vision that lay before us. I saw Tim Dickinson, our Battalion Chief, standing off by himself, and Garry and I approached him. Garry mentioned the fact that he was having doubts about staying and Tim said something that helped me to make up *my* mind right then and there. "Nobody has to stay that doesn't want to," he told us, "but I know what I'm going to do. I'm staying right here." I knew what he meant. In that simple statement he told me that this is *our* neighborhood. *My* neighborhood. Everyone else had, for the most part, already left. It's dangerous, but if you aren't willing to stay and try to defend your property and that of your neighbors, then, who will? I'm staying right here, too.

I looked back at the firehouse that we would use as shelter if this fire should burn over the highway. It was built from cinder block and had a metal roof. The plan was to deploy fire shelters inside the department and wait until the fire moved over the top of us. The fire shelters, known as "shake and bakes" to the wildland firefighters, are used exactly as the term implies. You shake them to open them up and then crawl inside, tucking it under your body, and staying in there until the fire burns over you or until you are dead, the first option being the most preferable. I figured the firehouse would be unlikely to burn and knew that we had bottles of oxygen should they be needed. Yep. I'm going to stay here and take my chances, along with everyone else who stays.

The fire would be coming over the ridge anytime now. The skyline was becoming a brighter orange color and the fireballs in the sky were now taking on a reddish hue. There was very little conversation going on among us. There was an occasional sob heard, but there was mostly silence as we watched the fire change a once-beautiful landscape into a disaster area.

Within a few minutes, the first finger of flame could be seen. It was surprisingly bright as it shot over the top of the hill. Soon, many other bursts of bright, orange fire could be seen, spewing over the ridge. Then, the flames began to go higher and higher until they were completely covering the skyline. Arms of fire shot hundreds of feet into the sky and, finally, we looked into the eyes of the monster that we had been fighting for five long days.

I was motionless. The fire was having a hypnotic effect on the people who were watching it. I told myself to remember this sight. This is something you will never, in your lifetime, see again. And I stood there, wide-eyed, and watched the fire come into Linden.

Chapter 18

As the fire roared over the top of the ridge, a hot, dry wind was blowing into our face. The smoky, acrid breath of this beast was nearly nauseating as I watched it devour the hillside. Then, a most remarkable thing happened. The wind began to shift. Instead of the furnace-like air coming off of the hill in front of us, a cooler wind began to blow in from behind us. If there are miracles in this world, then, I believed I was witnessing one at this moment. Nothing had gone in our favor from the time this fire was started. It had done as it pleased and had defied anyone or anything to stop it. But now, a gentle, cool breeze was blowing the flames back onto themselves, changing the face of the beast. The fire that, a few moments ago, was sending flames four and five hundred feet into the air, was now beginning to wilt. It was starting to lie down.

The people standing in the parking lot of the Linden Fire Department watched silently as the flames began to sink to the ground. We would not have to use the department as a shelter after all. The hillside, where the Chief's house was located, was still burning though, and some people were saying that they could see that her house was on fire. I think that Marilyn had become resigned to the fact that her house would be lost, and she quietly went up to her office to lie down.

She had previously retrieved some of her paintings (which she created) from her home, and they were scattered about the office. Until this fire, I had never known that Linden Fire Chief Marilyn Price was an artist, a painter specifically, and a fine one at that.

Out in the parking lot, I could see Terri Anderson, the only paramedic on our department, looking towards Marilyn's house with binoculars. She was leaning on a brush truck that had been brought out of the cinder pit to wet down the parking lot. She said she thought she could see the rafters of the Chief's house in flames, but could not be certain. It was decided that someone would take the brush truck up towards her house to get a firsthand look. They came back to the station a half an hour later with some remarkable news. The Chief's house was still standing! It is still not clear why it appeared to be on fire, but it was untouched and still inhabitable. We decided we should tell the Chief, so I walked up the stairs to her office. She was lying on a cot and appeared to be sleeping. "I'm not going to wake her," I thought. "Let her rest awhile and she will have some good news to wake up to for a change."

While one truck went to check on the Chief's house, another crew drove into Timberland Acres to get our first assessment of the damage that the fire had wrought in there. It was late, perhaps 10:30 or 11:00 p.m. when they came back to the station with their grim report. Many homes were gone. Incinerated. The firefighters who lived in T/A listened intently to the crew and learned the fate of their homes.

Nozzle's home was gone. Ed Dwyer's home was gone. Bob Filley's home was gone. Some homes had escaped unscathed, while others were mere ashes on the ground. Tim Heim's house was untouched as was C.D. Nunally's home. There was a stunned silence in the room as the Linden firefighters hugged their fellow firefighters who were now, homeless. There were no words to express the sorrow that we felt for our brothers. You are not in this alone, we told them, and we *will* help you through this.

After dawn broke, other crews, from several agencies (including the Forest Service) began arriving in T/A and they were calling for water tenders to be brought out to supply them with water for the fire engines. At 5:00 a.m. I was asked by the Chief to deliver a "bath tub" to Timberland Acres. I poured some coffee into a Styrofoam cup and went out to Tender 1, the oldest of the Linden Fire Department's water tenders, and cranked up the engine.

Garry was going to ride along with me, and we both loaded ourselves into the cab. The smoke at this hour of the morning was incredibly thick. I could barely make out the trees on the other side of the highway though they were less than a hundred feet away. I turned on the emergency lights of the old tender and pulled out onto the highway. The flashing red beacon on the roof was being reflected by the smoke, reminding me of the beam from a lighthouse in the fog.

As we got closer to the entrance to Timberland Acres, the smoke became more dense. I could hardly see the turn-off from Highway 260. The main road into T/A curves around like a snake, and with the smoke being so thick, I could drive at only five miles per hour. The scene was near ghostly. I was using the white line on the side of the road to guide me in. Visibility on the road was less than five feet as we inched down the highway in a gray fog. Occasionally, we would come upon a tree or a bit of brush that was still burning and the brilliant orange glow from the flames stood out in stark contrast to the black and gray environment. As the road gained in elevation, the smoke began to get less dense and we were able to see some of the destruction for the first time.

To say that this once lovely neighborhood looked like a war zone would be an inadequate description. While the smoke, for the most part, was gray and thick, some areas were still burning hot, and black smoke boiled up into the air. I came to the intersection where the bathtub was to be dropped and stopped the truck.

A bathtub is a large, square, rubber lining supported by a steel frame. Approximately three feet deep, it is used for dumping an entire tender-load of water in one place. The engines are equipped with a drafting system that allows them to draw water from the tub, thus, freeing up the water tender so it can be refilled.

It took both Garry and me to unload and set up the tub. Once it was in place, we got into the tender and started back to the station. It was getting brighter outside now and some of the devastation could be readily seen. In the area where we were, the fire had burned in a sporadic fashion. I looked off to the side of the road to where I knew a house had once stood. The house was completely gone. The block foundation was visible as was the charred and twisted remains of the metal roof, which had collapsed into the center of where the house had been. A bright, green side yard stood out in contrast to the blackened debris that had once been someone's home. There was a blue, plastic boat, still on a trailer, that had escaped the fire, though it was only twenty-five feet from the house. I could see that the power and phone lines were down and strewn alongside the road. I was pretty sure that the electric company had shut down the power into this area, but I steered well clear of the lines, just in case.

It was obvious that there were still many, many structures burning and smoldering further into the Timberland Acres neighborhood. Occasionally, we could see bright orange flames leaping up in the distance, but the head of the fire had moved out of T/A and further south, positioning itself for another possible run at Cheney Ranch. As I drove onto the main road out of T/A, the smoke had lifted enough to where I could see the asphalt and about thirty feet to each side of the roadway. The trees that twenty-four hours ago had been lush and green were now blackened sticks, their branches, like claws, reaching up to the sky. Some trees still had flames licking around their trunks while others had toppled over and lay smoldering on the ground.

I drove out of Timberland Acres with mixed emotions. I was stunned by what I had seen, but I knew that what I had witnessed was just the tip of the iceberg. There was sorrow for the people whose homes were burning, but there was also the feeling that we had a job to do. I guess this is the point where all of the training we have been through begins to kick in and you ignore the greater picture to focus on the task at hand. To contemplate the totality of this disaster would, I think, be too distracting to allow me to do a specific job, so I developed a sort of tunnel vision. There would be time enough to try and make sense of this fire later, but for now, safety, and trying to save whatever property was left, would have be the main points of focus.

Garry and I drove back to the Linden Fire Department main station in relative silence. The shock of seeing that neighborhood in ruins, and the many hours without sleep were beginning to take their toll.

Chapter 19

When we got to the station, I backed Tender 1 into a space by the highway. We walked inside to find dozens of boxes of Krispy Kreme doughnuts spread out on the tables. Someone had flown these in from Phoenix this morning. I had gone from near starvation to having to watch what I ate to avoid getting fat! Don Howard was there, getting ready for another morning briefing, so I grabbed a couple of doughnuts and a cup of coffee and sat down. I looked forward to these briefings because they put a face on this fire. Each day, the maps on the wall would change, showing the progress of the fire and each day the shape of the fire would change, also.

Don was pointing out some areas of concern on the map. There was a major back burn operation going on where the fire would approach Highway 60. The highway was a dividing line. To the east of the highway were the towns of Show Low and Pinetop-Lakeside. I was familiar with the area that he was pointing out. It was dense forest with very few meadows that could serve as a firebreak. The decision had been made to burn out the area closest to the highway to try to prevent the fire from jumping over to the other side. Don looked at the people gathered in the meeting room and said, "If this jumps Highway 60 and gets into the forest on the east side of the road, we will be looking at a million acre fire within days."

The hair on the back of my neck stood up. If that were to occur, the fire would burn all the way to New Mexico, relatively unimpeded. The thought of this fire, now named the Rodeo-Chediski Complex because the two fires had merged, running through the White Mountains was nearly unfathomable. It has already destroyed homes and fishing holes and other places not even known to me, and yet, it has shown no sign of abating. The fire, at last report, was still at zero-percent containment, meaning that there was not a line, anywhere, around the fire.

I began to wonder if there was really any way to stop this fire. It was going where it wanted to go and there wasn't a damned thing anyone could do about it. Though I have never been a religious man, at that moment, I said a silent prayer for something to help us in stopping the ongoing destruction of our homes and forest.

As if this bit of information was not depressing enough, a few minutes later, we learned of the death of one of our Linden volunteer firefighters. Sam Alexandre had been hospitalized in Phoenix, due to a lung infection. Sam was one of my neighbors and he and wife Della had become friends with Carol and me over the past couple of years. I believe Sam was in his seventies when he died.

The news of his passing left a darkened mood over the department. Could things possibly get any worse? It seemed as though everything that could possibly happen was happening. Bad news followed by worse news. I began to wonder if life would ever be "normal" again. Here I was, a former "city boy" who had volunteered on the fire department because I thought it was a good way to help out the community, caught up in the biggest disaster to ever hit the state of Arizona. For a brief moment, I felt totally overwhelmed by the circumstances in which I found myself. Then, I realized that I was no different than the rest of the people on the department. Some of us have had more training, or have been on the department longer but we were all facing a situation that was unique. No one had ever experienced a fire like we were facing now. That knowledge grounded me and helped me go on.

Later that day, we would have a group photo taken with all of the Linden Fire personnel standing in front of Engine 3. Because Sam had been an engineer on this fire truck, we placed his boots and helmet in front of the control panel to signify him as being a part of our department. God rest you, Sam. We will miss you.

It was decided that we were going to go back into Timberland Acres to help put out whatever hot spots we could find. Chief Price noticed that some of us were wearing hiking boots, which would melt if we tried walking through the bed of coals that was now T/A. She told us to go into Show Low and get some boots at the commissary. They would be billed to the department because, at this point, they would be vital firefighting equipment. Five of us loaded into Attack 1 and drove towards town.

As we came to the Show Low city limits, the roadblock was still in place. This time it was being manned by National Guard troops and they waved us through. They were heavily armed and had a no-nonsense look about them. This whole mountain had been declared a national disaster and that required calling out the guard. The family that had been at the roadblock the first time we went through was gone, but their banners and signs were still in place. I don't know how the other guys felt, but I appreciated this display of support from the community.

Driving through the now deserted streets of Show Low was somewhat eerie. The normally bustling community was a ghost town, save for the National Guard and the police vehicles roaming the streets. There were a few businesses still open, Safeway and K-Mart for example, that were catering to the needs of the emergency crews and the army of media people that were left in town.

Photo by Brian Buswell

Some of the crew from Linden Fire Department
Pictured from left to right (top row)
Tim Heim, Gary Roberts, Dewayne Saxton, Chief Marilyn Price, Sam Alexadres' boots
and helmet, Carol Lewis, Gary Holdcroft (myself), Ken Bantrum, Bill Vallery, Creig DeWitt,
Adam Hunter and Jack Travis.

Pictured from left to right (bottom row)
William "Wild Bill" Harris, C.D. Nunally, Ryan "Nozzle" Turner, Tim Dickinson, Eva
Dickinson, Troy Hvidsten, Don Harlacher, Erin Harlacher, Garry Moore and Art Johnson.
Not pictured are Terri Anderson, Eddie Morin and Bob Filley.

We turned onto Central Ave. and headed toward the high school. I had not expected the sight that awaited us. There was a phalanx of media trucks lining the street for several blocks. All had their satellite dish pointed to the heavens and their logo painted on the side of the large box vans. There were the local news crews from Arizona as well as national crews, such as CNN and FOX.

There was small tents set up on the campus grounds everywhere with sleeping bags and gear spread out next to them. Hundreds of people were milling about the area, all wearing the green pants and yellow shirts, common garb for the wildland firefighters. In the direction of the football field were several large tents being used as mess halls and several other, smaller tents that were selling various types of firefighting gear. The atmosphere was almost circus-like. If it weren't for the horrific clouds of smoke in the background, one would have thought that Barnum and Bailey were in town.

We parked the attack truck next to one particular tent and got out. It was a strange feeling to be in the midst of so many people after being out on the fire line. I could tell that for most of the firefighters, this was just another job. One more fire in a string of many that they had been on this year. I felt somewhat out of place wearing the orange jumpsuit and was glad that I was not the only Linden firefighter to be wearing one. I could tell by the looks from some of the people in the area that they thought we were the prison crew being brought in to help fight the fire. It was a bit humbling and I wanted to tell them, "Hey, see this logo? This is our department! This is our fight!" but it would not have accomplished anything. We stayed together as a group and walked into the tent.

This was almost like a street fair. Inside the tent were walls of boxes, each containing a different brand of boots. There were also T-shirts that had been printed with a "Rodeo-Chediski Complex" emblem. They had not wasted any time getting these on the market. I knew that most of the firefighters liked to keep these shirts as souvenirs from the fires they had been on, so I wasn't terribly surprised by seeing them. We were approached by a salesman and seated, almost immediately. We explained what we needed: good, heavy-duty boots that would not melt as we were walking through the embers. In no time, he had several boxes off of the rack and was telling us how the boots should feel when we put them on.

He had chosen "White's Smoke Jumper" boots for us. They were top of the line and highly sought after by professional wildland firefighters. I was astounded when he told us that they sold for $350.00 a pair, but the other guys seemed to take it in stride. He laced the boots onto our feet to show us the proper way of doing it and began to explain, "When you stand up, you should feel like you are standing on a roll of quarters. Now, these boots are going to be pretty stiff so you should unlace them and fill them (yes, the inside of the boot) with hot water. This will soften the leather. We recommend wearing them wet for the first few times you put them on." I was a bit incredulous. Put hot water into a $350.00 pair of boots? You have got to be kidding me! As long as I don't feel hot coals burning through the soles, they should be fine the way they are. I would, later, come to greatly regret not following this gentleman's advice.

I walked out of the tent wearing the new boots, carrying my old, comfortable boots in a box under my arm.

Hmmm. They do feel a bit stiff, alright. I figured I would get use to them as the days wore on.

We meandered around the school grounds for a while, looking at the latest maps that had been posted outside the media briefing area and taking advantage of the array of iced beverages, which were in tubs everywhere. There was a crowd of news people gathering at one of the buildings and we were hoping to see a live briefing, but it kept being postponed until the point arrived where we had to return to Linden.

Chapter 20

When we arrived back to the station, there was a group of firefighters standing in the middle of Highway 260, all of them looking off toward Juniper Ridge and the many smoke columns rising up from that area. It was beginning to seem as though this fire would become a permanent fixture in the White Mountains. At one point I thought to myself, "It's pointless to try and fight this fire." It was already being dubbed "The Monster" by the local newspaper, and it was living up to this moniker. If you stopped it on one flank it would rear up its head and start burning on two new flanks.

We were beginning to hear of a large amount of destruction in Heber-Overgaard, but to this point it was mostly conjecture. We heard that Bison Ranch had burnt to the ground. Bison Ranch is one developer's idea of an Old West prairie town. With wooden sidewalks and fake storefronts, it would be a firefighters nightmare if it did catch fire. We were also hearing that hundreds of homes and businesses were either burnt or burning and that the fire was making a forceful run at Forest Lakes, another small settlement of vacation homes right on Highway 260. This fire was impacting every community on the Mogollon Rim.

Several Linden personnel were already in Timberland Acres when I was instructed to take a water tender out there and tail Engine 2. Hot spots were everywhere and they would need huge amounts of water to extinguish them. Once again, Garry Moore and I would be the crew on Tender 1. We jumped into the truck and began driving up the highway towards T/A. Both of us were wearing the brand-new Smoke Jumper boots that we had acquired at the commissary in Show Low. I noticed, as I drove, that the tops of the boots, which came up to the middle of my shins, were beginning to rub the skin a bit. "When we meet up with Engine 2, I'll have to pull my socks up higher," I thought. I didn't know this at the time, but I was in the beginning stages of what is known to veteran wildland firefighters as "White Bites." An affliction caused by wearing a pair of new White boots, it is not fatal, but can make you wish you were dead. I would become very familiar with this condition as the day wore on.

We met up with Engine 2 and a brush truck on one of the roads behind the Linden Fire substation. I stopped the truck and got out to see what we were going to be doing. A house had obviously been at this location, but all that was left now was a smoldering pile of debris on top of a cinder block foundation. A swing set, still standing, gave testimony to the fact that a family with children had lived here. Ironically, there were still several plastic trucks and toys, scattered about the lot, that had escaped the flames and heat, while a few yards away, the house, where this family had lived, was devastated. The surrounding area had been badly burned but there were a few large oak trees that still had green leaves on them. The thin, scraggly pine trees had been obliterated by the fire, but if they were removed, and the lot cleaned up, this family may be able to rebuild here.

Though there was smoke still rising from the debris, we decided we would be better off looking for spots that were still hot enough to blow up into flames. With Engine 2 in the lead, we left this lot and drove up to where the fire had burned hottest. That would be the point where it initially entered Timberland Acres at the top of Juniper Ridge.

As I followed the fire engine through the winding roads in the subdivision, I realized that we were going to be going past the place where Ryan "Nozzle" Turner's house had once stood. We pulled up in front of his lot and all of the firefighters got out of their trucks. His home was burned to the ground. The fire had snaked its way to his house after burning his neighbors' house to the west. The path the fire had chosen was evident, yet baffling. The flames had crawled through the grass, went underneath a camping trailer that belonged to Ryan's dad, and then up the hill. It had ignited the wood siding of the home and continued to burn until there was nothing left. The camp trailer was spared as was another utility trailer parked nearby. One other thing had been spared also. In his front yard, out toward the street, a flagpole stood, still flying the American flag. It was reminiscent of the flag that had stood atop the World Trade Center during the disaster of 9-11. This was our own personal 9-11 and his flag would come to symbolize that fact. Later, a group of Linden firefighters would stand with Nozzle as he ceremoniously lowered the flag to half-staff.

Every time I drove past this flagpole, with the flag blowing in the wind, it would give me a sense of hope. All is not lost. Some things can survive the mightiest of disasters and give hope, however small, to the ones around it.

We turned the trucks around and drove back towards the substation. I had been deeply moved, standing in front of what was left of Nozzles' home. A seed of anger and resentment toward the fire had been planted and the only way to deal with it would be to try and save someone else's home from suffering the same fate as Nozzles. I would approach the task before me with a renewed vigor.

As we passed the sub-station, I could see that there were supplies of water and Gator-Aide placed inside the bay. The road curved up a steep hill and wound around the top of Juniper Ridge. Halfway up the hill, on the right side of the

Walking Through the Ashes 121

road, we could see a large amount of smoke rising up from an area where a cabin had once stood.

The view to our left was one of unspeakable destruction. We could see across a valley and all the way to the top of the ridge. Every tree had burned. There was no green from the conifers. There were no reds or yellows or blues from wildflowers. Those colors had been replaced with white, black and gray. I have heard this type of devastation referred to as a "moonscape" but I don't think that is an adequate description. It cannot capture the absolute loss of a forest. It does not take into consideration the birds and the other animals that lived here and, quite possibly, died here. It does not take into consideration the human dreams that were sent to the sky in the form of smoke and ash. It does not capture the concept of time, the hundreds of years it will take for this forest to regain its grandeur. It is, simply, an inadequate description of what happened here.

We pulled into the driveway where the smoke had been rising. The small cabin that once stood here was gone. In what was becoming an all too familiar sight, the only thing recognizable was the block foundation. The smoke was erupting from a pile of wood that had been stacked up along the side of the house. I'm sure it was used to feed the woodstove, which was lying on its side in the burned out shell. I could see a "Woodsman" logo on the stove and thought of my father's place in Pinetop.

He used to have a stove very similar to this one and I remembered how fond he was of it. He, too, had a large stockpile of wood, cut to size and ready to be burned when the weather called for it. The simplicity of heating your home with a wood fire, I think, is a notion that is deeply ingrained in the human consciousness. It is a steady, even heat source and it makes for a cozy evening when the snow and wind are blowing outside. The stove that I was looking at now has warmed its last home and heart.

Looking down into the remains of the cabin, I could see a set of blue porcelain canisters, largely unbroken, that once held flour and sugar or perhaps tea, in happier times. There were metal items that had been melted beyond recognition, but they were a treasure of some sort, to somebody, at one time.

I felt somewhat voyeuristic. Only fire crews and emergency personnel were being allowed into this area and I knew that whoever owned this property had no idea of its present condition. I could envision them, when allowed to return, sifting through the ash and burnt dreams, retrieving this or that, to set aside for a new cabin. Or, maybe they would simply have it all hauled away, being unable to face the magnitude of their loss.

It was obvious that the fire had come into this area full-force. The trees, burnt but still standing, showed burn patterns on their trunks that gave testimony to this fact. The bark on one side of the tree had burned cleanly away, exposing the white interior, and on the other side of the tree, the fire had left a snakeskin pattern on the bark where the flames had whipped around it. I would see this clearly defined, geometric pattern on nearly all of the trees in this area.

We soaked the woodpile with water and began loading the hose back onto the truck. I walked up to front of the driveway and saw a small metal rod sticking up out of the ground with two lengths of chain attached to it. It held a sign of some sort at one time. I could see that the sign was still there, facedown on the ground, having been blown off by the fierce wind when the fire blew through here. I picked it up and turned it over. There was a caricature of a man in a boat and the message "gone fishin'" written above. I thought of the irony of this moment. Here I was, standing in the smoldering rubble of this person's home, the blackened forest around me, holding this sign. Fishing seemed to be a long forgotten memory from the deep past. I would much rather be in a boat on some cool mountain lake, lounging the day away surrounded by water, than tromping around in this desolate scene of destruction. I hung the sign back on the pole and walked back to my tender.

The boots on my feet were starting to bother me. Every step I was taking was beginning to be a chore. I looked over at the tender to see Garry unlacing his boots. They were starting to get to him too. I thought that seemed like a good idea and sat down next to him and began unlacing my boots, also. As the laces relaxed, the flow of blood returned to my shins and ankles. The skin on my shins was bright red in several spots and I wished I'd had some bandages to apply where the boots were rubbing. I left the laces untied and wrapped them around my ankles. This helped a good deal and we got back in the truck and started up the road.

We got to the top of the hill and were at the spot where the Linden crew had come in with bulldozers and water tenders, before being thrown out by the Forest Service a couple of nights ago. The homes on the opposite side of the road were still there. They had green trees around them. What the crews had done in the short time they were in here had spared several families from having to deal with the loss of their homes. They would have to come to grips with the loss of the forest, but their homes were still standing.

I wondered how I would feel if I found my house still standing in the midst of a burnt forest. Was it not the forest that brought me to put my home here in the first place? I wished at that moment that we could somehow speed up time to see how long it will take for Nature to heal this forest. It will take more time than I have been allotted on this earth, I fear.

Rounding a bend in the road, we came across a hillside that had a few hot spots still smoldering. We jumped out of the tender and grabbed a couple of shovels and started up the hill. Oh God, but these boots are miserable! I got a few steps further and decided to try and hit the hot area with a water hose. I'm starting to get into a predicament here. The "White Bites" are getting worse and I'm not sure that hot coals wouldn't be preferable to what these boots are doing to my feet! Garry was going through the same thing. When the hot spots had been cooled, everyone decided to head back to the sub-station for lunch. Good idea, because I'm ripping these damned boots off of my feet as soon as we get there!

As the day heated up, I was starting to sweat. Because I was wearing jeans under the orange jumpsuit, my legs and feet were beginning to sweat as well. The perspiration was like putting salt on the areas that the Whites had rubbed raw. Every single step was one of sheer agony after a while. My God, what sadistic SOB made these boots? He should be forced to walk a mile, no ten miles, better yet, one hundred miles in these 100% leather implements of torture!

We came to the station and both Garry and myself found the nearest chairs, sat down and pulled those boots off of our feet. I peeled my socks off and started massaging my poor aching feet. Man, it's just the middle of the day. How in the world are we going to make it through the rest of the day, let alone the rest of the fire? I have never felt such a sense of relief as when those boots hit the floor without my feet in them. I stood up on the cool, concrete slab in the bay and savored the first bit of comfort I had had on my feet for hours. I would have but one hour to try and get my feet prepared to go back into the black boots of death and I didn't know if I could do it. I was going to have to psyche myself up for this feat of shear and utter terror. For right now though, I'm going to enjoy the feeling of being barefoot.

There was fresh fruit and submarine sandwiches for lunch, as well as a tubful of soft drinks. Water and Gator-Aide were the most preferable drinks while fighting the fire, but sometimes an ice-cold cola just can't be beat. I ate my lunch as slowly as I possibly could, knowing what awaited Garry and me. I couldn't fathom what it was going to be like, forcing those hideous black…things, back onto my, seemingly, mortally injured feet. When I saw that everyone was starting to stand and stretch, I knew that we were getting ready to head back out into the burn. Gingerly, inserting my toes into the boots and easing the rest of my foot down inside, I cursed Chief Price under my breath for sending us to the commissary to get these boots, which by now, were feeling like bear traps. Oh my, to be able to just sit, with my feet elevated and nowhere to go, nothing to do.

Oh well. Enough griping. I thought that I could bear the pain for a few more hours, because, after all, the people who lived in this neighborhood would gladly trade the pain of some tight boots in return for their homes being spared.

Garry and I got back into the tender and followed behind Engine 2. We stopped several times to extinguish various hot spots throughout T/A. I kept noticing one area of smoke just down the street from the station, and when we drove by it once again, I got on the radio to Engine 2 and suggested we check it out further.

The smoke was about fifty yards off the road and was coming from an oak stump that was still smoldering. We were able to reach it with a jump line. I don't recall who was manning the nozzle, but when they began to spray the stump, it started to hiss violently as the water mixed with hot embers. They began to shoot it with a straight stream to hit a particularly hot spot, when all of a sudden, the ground started to collapse around the base. The firefighters that had been standing nearby, jumped back a few feet, as smoke, ash and embers began flying into the air. The firefighter on the hose kept a stream of water aimed at the area that was collapsing and soon, the smoke and ash began to settle. We cautiously stepped forward to inspect the hole in the ground. It was nearly twelve feet deep and four feet across. The fire had incinerated the top of the huge, old oak tree and then burned down into the roots. All that was left of the tree was a bed of embers at the bottom of the pit. We continued to soak the bottom of the hole until it was no longer smoking and then we set up yellow "caution" tape to ward others away from this area.

We would find these pits everywhere in the burn area. Some of the hillsides in T/A were covered in manzanita. It's a low growing shrub that can get so thick that it is virtually impossible to walk through. It has bright red branches and green leaves and is notorious for burning at extremely high temperatures. Manzanita also has an extensive root system that can stretch for hundreds of feet away from the main body of the bush. I saw several instances where fire had continued burning through the roots of the plant, reappearing many yards away. I knew that this was going to be a problem for us. Even if the main body of the fire were put out, these hot spots would continue to reappear for weeks, if not months afterwards. We will be fighting the remnants of this fire for a long time to come.

After securing the area around the massive sinkhole, Garry and I hobbled back to the tender. Though I would not have wished the pain in my feet on anyone, I was secretly glad to have someone to commiserate with. The boots became a sort of running joke between us, each trying to outdo the other in describing the discomfort of wearing these ghastly shoes.

We received word on the radio that someone had spotted smoke behind a house that was situated high on a hill. We followed the engine up a winding, steep road that came to a dead end. The engine drove up to the house and asked us to stage the tender on the road until we were needed. The road up to the house was a steep incline and I wasn't sure that this old tender, with a full tank of water would even make it up there. I had to back up, pull forward, back up, pull forward several times until I had the water tender pointing back down the hill. I set the air brakes and we waited to hear from the crew up at the house.

From what we could hear on our radio, it appeared that the smoke was emanating from a fallen tree that was several yards away. While the structure, itself, was not being threatened, the crew decided to go ahead and soak the log with water. We sat in the cab for about thirty minutes while the crew above us worked on the smoldering tree. When they were satisfied that it was out, they started down the hill only to find that they couldn't make the turn in the driveway without moving another log that was in their way. This was going to require extra manpower. I heard Engine 2 calling for Tender 1 and answered them, praying that I wouldn't be called upon to climb the hill to the house in these boots. My prayer was answered when they asked for Garry Moore to come up. He is huskier than me and was the logical choice, or so I thought in my pain-addled mind. I have to say that I truly admired Garry as he jumped out of the cab and began trudging up the hill to help remove the log that was blocking the engine. I could not have done it without crutches, I do believe.

Chapter 21

After the engine was able to turn around, they gave Garry a lift down the hill to the tender. We were told that a Forest Service crew had run out of drinking water, and since the tender and the engine, both, had several cases of bottled water, we arranged to meet them at an intersection close to the sub-station. We pulled up and stopped at the meeting point and got out of the cab to await the arrival of the Forest Service folks.

As I looked around I could see that the fire had not burned in this immediate area with the same ferocity as it had just up the hill. I could tell that it had burned extremely hot but the flames seemed to have spared many of the trees in this area. The pine tree's boughs, though unburned, had been frozen in time, their branches pointing in the direction that the fire had been moving. I'm sure that they will not survive. By most estimates, the fire was burning at over 2,000 degrees Fahrenheit when it came through here. It seemed that the trees had undergone a sort of reverse freeze-drying process, being flash dried by heat instead of cold.

I saw something off to the side of the road and walked over to examine it. In a sad example of what had occurred here, I saw that it was the body of a large squirrel, partially buried in the ground. Its fur had been singed slightly but it appeared to be in good shape otherwise. It looked to me as though the poor thing had tried to dig a hole to escape the oncoming fire and had expired before it could get the hole deep enough. I pointed it out to Creig Dewitt, a lieutenant on Linden Fire, and he said he thought it had died of asphyxiation rather than the heat. When the fire moved over this area it had sucked the oxygen from the air. The combination of heat, smoke and lack of oxygen was simply too much for this creature. I was sure that this scene had been played out in many other areas of this, now decimated, forest. The thought of this squirrel, desperately trying to dig his way to safety, would gnaw at me for a long time to come. To this day, it bothers me to think about it.

The Forest Service crew soon arrived and we offered them several bottles of water, which they accepted gratefully. Leaning against the engines, we stood there chatting for a while, exchanging stories of what we had seen and done so far. The Forest Service crew (there were only three of them) was a fairly rag-tag looking group. You could hardly tell that they were wearing the yellow and green wildland gear, as they were covered in soot from head to toe. This was the general appearance of nearly everyone on this fire. There was no way to escape being covered in the ash and greasy soot because it was everywhere. After saying goodbye, we decided to go further up the road we were on. The road climbed up a hill and would give us a view from the other side of the canyon that we had been looking across when we were putting out the fire in the woodpile earlier. We knew that there were, or had been, several houses at the top of this rise and went to check this area for hot spots.

Reaching the top of the hill, we could see that the fire had been fairly merciless when it burned through here. A large, elegant, split-level home that had once stood here was now a smoking heap of debris. Ironically, a large, nearby, house under construction had been left untouched. The house was framed out and the white 2x6 studs and rafters stood out like bleached bones against the backdrop of the burned trees. The owners would have the option of continuing to build.

The incomplete house sat on what is probably one of the highest points in Timberland Acres and, before the fire, would have had unobstructed views all around. It would have looked out on the foothills of T/A and the Linden valley to the northeast, and to the south would have been a vast expanse of Forest Service and Apache Reservation land, with a mottled carpet of pine and oak trees. The view now, however, is much different and I wondered if, after seeing the new panorama, the owner would proceed with building this house.

There were several hot areas around the two-story house that had burned and we focused our attention on them. There had been two or three recreational vehicles parked around the now smoldering house, and they had all been burnt. Save for the frames, they were nearly unrecognizable. As we walked amid the ruins of what had once been a beautiful home, I saw that several plastic hummingbird feeders were hanging from the branch of a tree, still filled with liquid. My guess is that the sweet nectar they contained is what kept them from being consumed by the flames. The shape of the plastic bottles was a bit distorted, but they had survived. I don't think they are going to be used for quite a while though.

We trudged around, spraying any smoldering spots that we could find, when our radios began chattering. The Forest Service was calling an end to operations in here for the day, and all crews were being told to stage at Timberland Rd. and Highway 260. I was more than ready to leave. My feet were killing me. We met up with several fire crews at the intersection and, after getting a short briefing on the days progress, were dismissed. Because we had been working in an area that was under Forest Service jurisdiction we were, technically, working for them and they had the authority to say when it was time to go to work and when it was time to quit.

Chapter 22

I pulled the tender out onto Highway 260 and drove towards the Linden Fire Department. I was getting hungry, I was tired and I wanted to get these boots off of my feet. After parking the truck, Garry and I walked into the east bay and I could see that a buffet line, of sorts, had been set up. People were in line for what appeared to be some good grub. There were three older gentlemen, in aprons, dishing up pork chops, mashed potatoes with gravy, fresh green beans and the biggest, fluffiest biscuits I had ever seen. There were pans of sweet cantaloupe and watermelon along with a variety of cold beverages. These guys knew how to cook! I consider myself to be a good cook. I know my way around a kitchen pretty well but these three guys were putting my abilities to shame. From what I could gather about them, they had cooked for trail rides and cattle drives in their earlier days and had obviously not lost their talents. I grabbed a plate and stood in line for what was the best meal I had eaten in a long time.

After dinner, I walked out into the parking lot. During one her trips to town, Carol Lewis had picked up a carton of "Swisher Sweets Little Cigars" for me and after the meal I had just had, a smoke would hit the spot. I saw Tim Heim leaning against his pick-up truck and walked over to him. I suggested that since the fire was not going to threaten Linden tonight, we should drive his truck over to my house. I have a three-bedroom house and would be able to accommodate a few firefighters for the night, if they wanted to sleep in a real bed. Nozzle walked up to us and I told him that he would be welcome, as well.

Tim and I drove to the house in his truck and Nozzle followed in his own vehicle. I opened the front door and was, once again, glad that I had left the air-conditioner running. Tim and Nozzle, both, noticed the fresh smelling air immediately. Carol and I had been planning to have a few people over to our house before the fire had started and, as luck would have it, I had a case of long neck bottles of beer in the refrigerator. Because my neighborhood was one of the few that still had electricity, the beer was nice and cold. I told Tim and Nozzle to help themselves to the beer and went into the bedroom to peel off the coveralls, which now seemed like a second skin. After removing the dreaded black boots from my feet, I walked into the kitchen to find both guys with a beer in hand. I poured myself a glass of whiskey (over ice, with a splash of water!) and filled a pan with hot water. I set the boots on the ground and filled them to the top with the water and the three of us went to sit on the front porch.

This was the first time we had been able to sit down and actually ponder the occurrences of the last few days. The knowledge that Ryan's home had been destroyed hung in the air like a phantom. I told him that he and his fiancée, Brandi, would be welcome to stay in our spare bedroom until they figured out what to do. He reluctantly accepted the offer.

The topics were varied as we talked of the things that we had seen and done while on the fire line and, after three drinks, we called it a night. We needed a good night's sleep and this would be the first opportunity that any of us had had for five days. I went to my bed and fell asleep almost instantly. Nozzle slept on the hide-a-bed in the den and Tim took the spare bedroom. I had been asleep for, perhaps, three hours when I heard the sound of footsteps running down the hallway, followed by the sound of the front door slamming. Nozzle had awakened in the middle of a dream and a bad one at that. I could hear him yelling "fire, fire" and I got out of bed and went outside to check on him.

This was not the first such dream he'd had like this. Days earlier at the fire department, before his home had burned, he'd awakened from a similar dream and was shouting something about fire. At that time, he had taken a ribbing from the people around him who were sleeping on cots. I didn't know if this was the beginning of a pattern for him, but I was concerned that he was internalizing his thoughts and emotions about this fire. I thought to myself that I should, at the least, mention this to the Chief. I didn't know if there were counselors available at this stage of the fire, but it was obvious to me that Ryan was going to have to talk to someone who could help him deal with the anxiety that this blaze was causing him.

I stepped out on the front porch. "Hey dude, are you OK?" I asked. I could tell that he was starting to wake up and that he was slightly embarrassed by his actions.

"Yeah…yeah, I'm OK," he mumbled. We walked back into the house and went back to bed. This damned fire was insidiously snaking itself into our lives in ways that I couldn't have imagined. I lay there for most of the night, expecting to hear the front door slam again at any minute.

I got out of bed early the next morning and, after showering, went to the kitchen to make some breakfast for the three of us. I had to roust Tim out of bed. I swear, that boy could have slept through the whole fire had he had a comfortable enough bed and no one to wake him. I guess the smell of frying bacon overrode his need for sleep, because he came ambling into the kitchen looking for coffee. Nozzle was already up and sitting at the table, lacing up his boots. "Sorry about last night," he said, sheepishly, "that dream was so real…it just…. I don't know."

"Don't worry about it," I told him. "We're all dealing with this damned fire in different ways. At least you had your pants on." I tried to inject a bit of humor into the situation. This fire was a long way from being over and we all would have to handle the consequences the best we could.

I put a pan of potatoes and onions on the stove and went outside to see how the boots had fared after soaking in water overnight. I emptied them out and could feel that they were noticeably softer. My feet, though tender, had only one blister, that being on my small toe. I put a band-aid over the toe and found a pair of heavy wool socks to put on. I was going to have as much cushioning as I could between my feet and the boots. The places where my skin had been rubbed raw were still quite painful. I pulled the socks up as high as I could and put the boots back on my feet. Though still damp, the boots felt more supple, and I thought that they might be bearable. I made a mental note to repeat the water treatment again tonight, if I could.

It was 7:00 a.m. when we finished breakfast. I locked the house up and we drove back to the station. The fire, though still in Linden, was burning slower than it had been. Smoke was starting to rise up in a neighborhood known as Fools Hollow Ranch, and I assumed that this area was going to be the focal point for today.

When we arrived back at the station, there were several firefighters in line, waiting for breakfast in the east bay. Though we had just had breakfast at *my* house, I grabbed a plate and took my place in line with the rest of the guys. The three gentlemen who had been dishing up the great suppers were cooking again and I could see that biscuits and sausage gravy were on the menu this morning.

I struck up a conversation with the man who was in charge of making the biscuits. I have tried and tried, but I have never been able to make biscuits that were as big and fluffy as his. A thin, gray haired old cowboy, he listened to my idle chatter and could tell I was trying to winnow his recipe from him. He was not going to give it up. He looked at me as if to say "Ah ha, after me lucky charms, eh?" I swore to myself that I would get him to divulge his secret before this fire was over. He would prove to be a tough nut to crack.

Chapter 23

Don Howard was getting ready to do another morning briefing and after finishing off my plate, I sat and listened. The burnout operations had apparently been successful out on Highway 60 but there was still great concern about the wind shifting and blowing the flames across the roadway. This was on the Apache Reservation and Rick Lupe's Fort Apache Hot Shot crew was trying to contain the fire in this area. *Our* task today would be to scour the neighborhoods in Linden to find any structures that may still be burning or any hot spots that would need attending. I would be assigned to drive Tender 3 with orders to tail Engine 3 so they would have a good supply of water, should they need it.

Though I am familiar with, and can operate all three of our water tenders, Tender 3 is my favorite. It is the newest of all the tenders and is faster and more up to date. The tank is bright red and the cab of the truck is white, with great orange flame decals rising up from the grill. Another amenity on this tender that the other tenders do not have is air-conditioning. Driving this truck is going to put a whole new face on chasing down the fire's remnants.

After a crew was assigned to Engine 3, we loaded the vehicles with bottled water and Gator-Aide, checked our water levels and then headed out to patrol the neighborhoods. Because it was still early and the fire was not yet up and running, we decided to check the neighborhoods on the north side of the highway. The fire had not jumped Highway 260 in this area, but we were concerned that it may have sent some firebrands ahead of itself and did not want to give it a chance to get a foothold on this side of the road. Some Forest Service officials had already predicted that the fire would not only cross the highway in our district, but would burn all the way to the Show Low Airport, some six air miles from Linden.

The first area to be patrolled was the Chaparral subdivision. Similar to Timberland Acres in the fact that it has one road in and one road out, it has very thick vegetation and a high density of homes in a small area. The smoke was still quite heavy and we drove with our overhead emergency lights on to enhance our visibility to other traffic. I stayed about twenty yards behind the engine as we pulled onto Chaparral Road and drove slowly through the subdivision. Strange to see this neighborhood deserted. Normally, it would be bustling with people raking their yards or tending to their gardens, but it's a virtual ghost town this morning. Because the homes are situated in a bowl-shaped draw, the smoke would tend to accumulate more readily in here than it would in a more flat environment and visibility was poor.

I could see that several large trash bins had been knocked over and the garbage thoroughly spread around it. These were big, heavy bins and I doubted that a dog was responsible for this. More likely, a black bear had taken advantage of, what would seem to him as, a veritable buffet. We saw no fire or obvious hot spots in here and decided to go over to the Fool Hollow Ranch Estates. We knew there would be fire left in there because the smoke was still rising, and had been, for two days now.

I followed Engine 3 back onto Highway 260 and tailed them to the turnoff to Fools Hollow Ranch. All of the roads in this subdivision are named after poker terminology. There is Full House Lane, Deuces Wild Road, Aces High Drive, etc. Trying to find your way around in here can be rather tricky if you are relying on the street names. We turned onto Full House Lane, which is the main road into the area, and began winding our way towards the back of the neighborhood. We came to Deuces Wild Rd. and turned right. We could see orange flames on the ground at the end of the street and, as if that weren't reason enough to go back here, one of our full-time firefighters lived on this road.

Kevin Marie lived in a large, sprawling house on a hill overlooking the spot where we were seeing fire. He was from Jersey (the island, not the state) and lived here with his mother and father. He is a tall, burly fellow with an accent that is not quite English and not quite Scottish. Because he was a carpenter before he was hired onto the Linden Fire Department, I suspected that he would have his place fairly secured. We drove up the driveway to check on his home and found that he had placed four sprinklers on his rooftop and had them running full force. His home was thoroughly soaked and water was running from the roof to the ground and out onto the road. I doubted that his home would be in jeopardy from firebrands falling on his roof or in his yard because everything was wet. We turned our attention to the fire we saw on our way in here.

The flames were, indeed, on the ground. While Engine 3 went further up the road to check for hot spots, I pulled the tender up in front of the house that was closest to the actual fire.

I recognized this house as one that I been to, on a previous call, a couple of years ago. A young man had, allegedly, tried to commit suicide by shooting himself, but when we got on scene we found that the wound was in his back, near his shoulder. It was a rather strange spot for a person to shoot himself, if this were, indeed, a suicide attempt. After securing the victim to a backboard, he was placed in an ambulance and the scene was turned over to law enforcement.

I never did hear of the ultimate outcome of this particular incident.

The fire turned out to be several tree stumps that had burned almost to the ground. There was just enough wind to breathe life back into the flames and they were flickering in several spots behind the home. Looking around, I could see that the main body of the fire had come dangerously close to the house. Though it hadn't burned, the scenery around it had been forever changed. This was becoming an all too familiar scenario. I pulled the red jump line from the tender and, after charging the line, was able to knock down most of the flames. I soaked the surrounding area so that the fire would not be able to creep any further. We would probably have to get a crew back in here later, with some hand tools to cut a line around the house.

My neighbor, Dewayne Saxton, was on Engine 3 and, after we had secured the home on Deuces Wild, said he wanted to check on his boss' property, which was located nearby. Dewayne is a Park Ranger when he is not fighting fire and his supervisor had asked him to drive by his acreage, if it were possible, and let him know how it had fared. As was becoming the norm, Dewayne's boss' property had sustained heavy fire damage and still had active fire in a few places. Once again, we pulled the fire hose off of the truck and trudged back into the hot area to put down what was left of the previous nights inferno. There were several areas of fire on this property, stubbornly refusing to be put out, and it would take us two hours to finally get the upper hand.

Deciding to break for lunch, we got back into our vehicles and drove to the station. Before I parked Tender 3, I pulled it underneath the downspout to top its tank off with water. When the tank was full, I parked the tender and went into the east bay.

The "delicate" aroma of hamburgers and hotdogs filled the air. I could see the wiry old cowboy, whose biscuit recipe I wanted, in the corner. He could see me too, and he kept positioning himself so I couldn't get to him. If he thinks he's going to get off of this fire without giving me that recipe, well, he's got another thing coming. The very least I can do is to eat some more of his chow. If he sees that I am truly enjoying his cooking, maybe he'll take pity on me and toss me that recipe. If not, well, there are other ways to make you talk, old man!

Even though the cowboy was pretty much ignoring me, I still ate two hamburgers. I grabbed a soda and walked towards the meeting room. I glanced over his way looking like a sick pup, but he was having none of it. Damn!

In the meeting room, Battalion Chief Tim Dickinson and Assistant Chief Eddie Morin were getting a crew together to go to the hillside by Chief Price's home. The hill had been covered in manzanita before the fire and there were some persistent hot spots that needed to be extinguished up there. I volunteered to go and jumped in Brush 702 with several other firefighters. We drove out to the base of the hill and began pulling hoses up to the area where we would be working.

The hill was steep and rocky. I could feel heat emanating from the soil and I knew that there would be embers smoldering several inches, if not feet, below ground. The hose line that we were pulling was smaller than the regular fire hose on the engines. It was the type used by the Forest Service when they are conducting prescribed burns or mopping up after a wildland fire. After the hose was in place we charged the line and began spraying water over the area. As soon as the water touched the soil, it began hissing and sputtering. There were still hot spots all over this hill. While two people manned the hose line the other guys would rake the ground with shovels and Pulaski's, exposing embers with every turn. Because the ground was gray with ash, it was difficult to tell which areas were still hot and we ended up dragging several lengths of hose through the coals, burning holes in them.

I was manning the hose, at one point, on a very steep portion of the hill. It was difficult to maintain a steady footing and I kept sliding backwards on the loose scree. During one of these freefalls, I saw a flash of light from a piece of metal on the ground. I bent down and picked it up and saw that it was a badge. My badge. I had received it just a few months before this fire had started. I was wearing it, clipped to my belt underneath the coveralls, so as to have a means of identifying myself as we went through the roadblocks in town. It must have come off of my belt and slid down the pant leg of the coveralls and then onto the ground. It was simply a stroke of luck that I had seen it and I knew that, had I moved a few feet either way, it would have been lost forever. I unzipped the coveralls and stuck the badge deep into my pant's pocket.

After thoroughly spraying and digging around the base of the smoldering trees, we regrouped at the top of the hill. From here, we could see just how close the fire had come to Marilyn's house when it came into Linden a few nights ago. I gauged it to be about fifty yards from her front door. It was no wonder that several people had thought that they were seeing her house on fire. The manzanita would have burned with an intensity that would have sent flames fifty-plus feet up in the air. It was a close call but her home was still standing, untouched by the fire.

From our vantage point on this hill we could look out over the Linden valley. We could see the fire department and the middle school. The problem was, we could not see behind us and we knew the fire was still very active someplace just over the ridge. There was concern among the crew that, perhaps this wasn't the safest place to be. We should, at the least, have a lookout stationed on a higher peak to warn us if the fire started to make another run into the area. Assistant Chief Eddie Morin was adamant that the fire would not run back through here because the mountainside between the active fire and us had already been burnt. He made a good point, but we were all still a little skittish from having watched the fire roar over this very hill. However unlikely it would be to reappear in this same spot, we knew that we could not outrun the fire should it make another pass at us.

Several firefighters were beginning to question Eddie's judgment. I understood their concern. Yes, there were still a few hot areas left on this hill, but extinguishing them was not worth someone getting hurt. Not only could we not see behind us, but also there were several helicopters working this hillside, each with a five hundred gallon bucket of water dangling from a line below it. Should they happen to not see us and drop their load, the falling water could hit us.

We started to see a good bit of smoke rising from an area below us and went to check on it. This would place us closer to the trucks and afford us an opportunity to get out of there should the fire reappear.

Besides the firefighters on this crew, we also had with us a Forest Service sawyer, who was remarkably skilled at cutting down trees. I don't remember his name but he was large, husky young man. What stands out in my mind was watching him walk up the steep terrain while lugging two chainsaws, one over each shoulder. I don't recall seeing him break a sweat. He worked very hard and was a valuable asset for the type of job with which we were faced. Not only would he be able to cut a path for us, if need be, but after we put out the fire in a tree, he could cut it down and allow us to fully soak the wood.

We located the smoke. It was in a stand of pinion pine and there was flame showing in the midst of them. They were in a draw and there was house about a hundred yards below. The fire in this draw was being very stubborn. There had been a crew out here previously and they had been putting out hot spots in this very same location. Wind was channeling through here and any unextinguished ember would burst into flame with the slightest breeze. We would work in here for a couple of hours before taking a break for lunch.

We went down to the house below us and sat down to rest. I was beginning to sense a sort of mutiny occurring. Several of us were ready to get off of this hill until we had a better idea of where the fire was located, while others were willing to stay and take their chances. As we were sitting there, sipping water and Gator-Aide, a vehicle pulled up in the driveway. It was Don Howard. He'd heard that there was a crew back here and came to check on us. He told us that, in his opinion, this was not the safest area for us to be. Yes, the fire *had* burned the hill behind us, but there were fingers of vegetation that had been untouched. It was not out of the question for the fire to re-ignite in these pockets of trees and make another run over the hill. If that occurred, we would not be able to see it coming until the last minute. "Do you have any lookouts on the hill above you?" he asked Eddie. When he was told there were none, he said, "Well, if you are going to stay back here, I would advise you to get someone up there.

You may want to wait for this area to cool down a bit and come back in here later."

I respected Don Howard's opinion and judgment. He had not given us one bit of bad advice so far and I couldn't see that happening now. When Eddie Morin chose to ignore Don's advice and return to the hillside without posting a lookout, I decided that it was time to find another assignment. We called on the radio for a truck to come and pick up those of us who wanted to leave.

Eddie is a dedicated firefighter and I would never, under normal circumstances, question his judgment. I thought that stress and lack of sleep were beginning to take their toll on him, however, and I would feel safer with someone else calling the shots. When the pick-up truck pulled into the driveway, a few other firefighters and I got in and headed back to the firehouse.

Chapter 24

A few days earlier, while working on this fire, I had developed an abscessed tooth. I'd had a root canal done on the tooth about six months prior and it had not bothered me since. Now it was becoming swollen and uncomfortable. I told Carol about this during a phone conversation and she contacted my dentist in Snowflake to get some medication for me. I drove Rescue out to the intersection of White Mountain Lake Road and Highway 77 to meet Carol and to retrieve the medication.

I pulled into the vacant parking lot of a business and stepped out of the truck. This was the first time we had seen each other in six days and we hugged and kissed for awhile before ever saying anything. Carol could not believe the amount of soot and ash covering me from head to toe. I retrieved the antibiotics from her and told her I had to go. They needed all the fire equipment they could get, back at the fire line. It was a brief rendezvous but it allowed us to see each other for a few minutes. In a bittersweet moment, I drove away wishing that she could be on the seat beside me.

After returning to the station from the hill near Marilyn's house, I decided that I would drive out to White Mountain Lake to spend the entire evening with Carol. I needed a break from this fire. It was beginning to wear on me and I wanted to have a few hours away from the destruction, a few hours when I would not have to think about it. I told Tim Heim, who was currently the IC for our department, and Chief Price, that I was going to leave the district for the evening but that I would be back first thing in the morning. Because we were basically doing a mop-up operation now, they agreed to allow me to go.

I went to the cinder pit where my truck was located, got in and started driving towards Show Low. I was less than a mile away from the station when a Navajo County Sheriff's deputy pulled behind me and turned on his overhead lights. I pulled off to the side of the road and rolled down my window. The deputy approached my vehicle and asked what I was doing in this area. Now, I was wearing a cap with the Linden Fire insignia printed on it, a blue t-shirt with the same insignia, the orange coveralls (now unzipped to my waist) that had "Linden Fire Department" written on it in several places, I had the orange placard on my dash and I was covered with ash and soot. I thought that the answer would be obvious, but I told him that I was with Linden Fire and that I was leaving the district for a while.

The officer looked tired, with dark bags under his eyes and a certain edginess in his voice that told me that he was not going to take any crap. I was not in the mood for any crap myself. I was close to the point of exhaustion, I had seen more destruction and tragedy in the last few days than I had seen in my entire life and I didn't like the idea of this deputy playing games with me.

He didn't have much to do because the fire was beginning to wind down in Linden. He was on the lookout for looters in the abandoned neighborhoods and when they didn't materialize, he decided to stop any private vehicle driving on the highway. After I told him that I was on the fire department, he started looking through the windows of my truck and saw the belongings that I had retrieved from my home, earlier. "What's all this stuff, then?" he asked. I explained to him that I thought that my house was going to burn to the ground when the fire made its run into Linden and this "stuff" was all that I had been able to save. He stood at the driver's side window and stared me in the eye.

I couldn't figure this guy out. I thought that we were on the same side, you know, protecting life and property and that kind of thing, but he had some sort of problem with me being in this area. "You have any I.D. on you?" I unclipped my badge from my belt and handed it to him. "This has my fire department I.D. number on it and if you like, we can go to the Linden Fire Department and Chief Price, herself, can tell you who I am and what I'm doing out here," I replied. I was being as polite as I could under the circumstance because I could tell that this guy was gunning for some sort of confrontation. He stared at me for a few more seconds and then returned my badge. Without saying anything else, he walked back to his vehicle, got in and made a u-turn.

This was an unusual occurrence. For the most part, everyone involved with this fire had worked as a team. Even though we had doubts about the Forest Services' plan to fight the fire; law enforcement, firefighters and Forest Service employees were working hand-in-hand trying to contain the blaze and keep everyone safe. The actions of this deputy made no sense to me.

I began to wonder if I would be able to make it to White Mountain Lake. There were at least two more roadblocks ahead of me.

I made it through the other roadblocks with no problems! I was asked for my I.D. and waved through. I drove through the deserted streets of Show Low and turned onto Highway 77 towards White Mountain Lake Road. There is a high spot on the highway that looks out onto the Linden valley and there was a crowd of people, pulled off to the side of the road, scanning the horizon with binoculars. The smoke from here was still very visible, as the fire was creeping up behind Show Low. I couldn't blame them for being curious. It took me a while to find the house where Steve, Cindy and Carol were staying, but when I pulled up in front of the place I was greeted like a hero returning from battle.

The first thing I wanted to do was to get the boots off of my feet and out of the orange coveralls. I went to the washroom and cleaned the soot and ash from my face and then sat down on the front porch with my wife and my friends. There was a drink waiting for me. A heavy sigh escaped my lips as I took in this respite from fighting the fire. Carol was full of questions and when Steve said, "Hey, just let the guy relax for a while," I was very grateful. I could tell her about the many things I had seen and done in the morning, but for right now, I simply wanted to relax.

I could tell that the atmosphere in the house was a bit tense. Carol told me that Steve was having a problem with our cats and that he had made the suggestion that they stay in the bedroom that Carol had been sleeping in. I could sympathize with him. Siamese cats are notorious for being very vocal. Hell, they bug me sometimes and I live with them permanently. I asked Carol to be patient with him. This is a huge inconvenience to everyone, but we will make it through and things will eventually get back to normal. After a couple of drinks, Carol and I went upstairs to the bedroom.

Carol had been very concerned about Coco, our chocolate point Siamese. She had not eaten or used her litter box since they had been evacuated. I went over to her, picked her up and began petting her. She started to purr loudly. I could feel that she had lost some weight from not eating but her nose was cold and she seemed to be healthy. I got undressed and stretched out on the queen-sized air mattress that Carol had brought from home. Coco would not leave my side. I put my arm around Carol, kissed her goodnight and fell asleep immediately. I can't remember when I have ever slept as soundly as I did that night. It was a deep, velvety sleep and I awoke in the morning feeling renewed. Refreshed. I heard the sound of crunching and looked over to see Coco eating her first food in a week.

Carol and I lay in bed for a while and I told her of a few things that had happened. I told her about Ryan and Brandi's home burning and that I had extended an invitation for them to stay with us. She readily agreed and that lifted a small burden from me. I did not want her to be overly worried about me, so I didn't tell her of the close calls in Pinedale or how the fire had roared into Linden. I did tell her that I thought that our home would be safe from this point on, but there was still a lot of active fire in the area.

Though Carol had brought a police scanner from home, they had been glued to the televised fire updates from Jim Paxon. They were glad to hear some first-hand information, however, so I told Steve that, although my house appeared to be safe, his home could still be threatened. He needed to be aware that the fire had not yet made a run into Show Low. While Carol and Cindy made breakfast, Steve and I sat on the front porch, drinking coffee. I told him again how grateful I was to him for opening up this house to Carol and our pesky cats. He shrugged it off, but I knew that the past few days had been very trying for him.

We had a fine breakfast of bacon, eggs and hash-browned potatoes. I drank another cup of coffee and looked out on the horizon towards Linden. The smoke was laying down in this neighborhood and it made the horizon look as if it were far, far away. I have to get back to Linden. I gave my word that I would be back first thing in the morning and I intend to keep it. I told Steve and Cindy goodbye, and then Carol and I walked out to my truck together. "You'll be home soon," I told her. "I think the fire is pretty much done with Linden. My guess is that you'll probably have to stay here for a few more days." I could tell that she wanted to come home. *Now.* We both knew that that was out of the question, though. I kissed her and said goodbye, giving a long honk of the horn and waving as I pulled away from the house. Looking in my rear-view mirror, I could see Carol standing there, watching me drive away.

Chapter 25

I decided to take the back road into Linden. Lone Pine Dam Road skirts around Show Low and would shave several miles from my commute back to the station. There was another roadblock set up at the Lone Pine-Highway 77 intersection and, again, I was asked for my I.D. and, again, I was waved through. I would guess it to be about eight miles from this intersection to my home in Linden. I would later learn that my neighbor, Fred Hathaway, who lives across the street from me, would cover these eight miles on foot to go and check on his home. He told me that he felt confident that his home would survive because he had firefighters living on either side of him, but he needed to see the condition of his house, firsthand. He also told me about shooting a garbage bag with his pistol, thinking it was a black bear standing before him, but that is as far as I will go with that story.

I decided to stop at my house and put some water on my trees. It had been several days since I had been able to water them and I was sure that they would be parched, if not dead. Driving down my road, I saw that the water sprinkler on my neighbor's roof was still on. The pressure was so low that the sprinkler had stopped oscillating. Water was pooled in his front yard and running back behind his house. I stopped my truck and went into his yard to turn off the faucet. As of now, our neighborhood appeared to be safe from the fire and the water pouring off of his roof was being wasted. His water bill had to be skyrocketing. I reached down to shut the hydrant off and saw that he had removed the handle, making it impossible to turn off. I went home and found a cap to screw on the end of the hose. This would stop the water from running for a while, but the hose itself would likely break after a while from the pressure being exerted on it.

I went to my house and started soaking our two maple trees. One was badly wilted, the other looked dead. I left the hose in the tree well and went to check on my garden. Before the fire started, it was lush and green. I had planted tomatoes, green chiles, squash, beans and melons. I was dismayed to see most of the plants badly wilted. The squash was probably dead and the tomato plants were not far behind. I did not have enough time or water pressure to soak the garden, so I walked away from it, thinking there still may be enough days left in the season to replant. After watering the trees, I drove back to the Linden Fire Department.

I felt good this morning. I had slept soundly, had a wonderful breakfast and was able to see that Carol and our cats, though stressed, were OK. Sitting down with Tim Heim to see what we would be doing today, I found that, once again, I would be assigned to drive Tender 3 behind the engine. We would check on the Fools Hollow Ranch area again and then go out to Burton, which is a bedroom community of Linden. After another cup of coffee and a doughnut, the crew of Engine 3 loaded up and drove into Fools Hollow, with me following in the tender.

We drove to the rear of the neighborhood and started working our way back to the highway. We checked on Kevin's house, it appeared to be in good shape, and then checked the house across the street where we had seen flames a couple of days ago. Though there were still small pockets of smoke in here, the area seemed to be fairly secure. Unless there was a drastic change in the direction of the wind, this region had seen the worst of the fire. We continued to drive, slowly, through the houses in here, looking at each home for signs of smoke.

As we snaked our way back to the highway, we came across a film crew. They were with the Animal Planet cable television station and been granted access to the area to shoot a documentary on how pets and livestock were coping with this disaster. They trained their cameras on the engine and tender as we drove by. I looked over at the home that seemed to be the focus of their attention and saw an animal control officer trying to lasso a snarling Rottweiler. "Good luck, buddy," I thought. "I'd rather be fighting this fire than trying to contain that beast." We waved to the camera and then drove onto Highway 260.

We had been receiving reports of smoke in the Burton area. The fire had crossed the highway near Juniper Ridge, but we hadn't heard of it running into Burton. We drove down the dirt road leading into the area and scanned the horizon as went. Though there are relatively few Ponderosa pines back here, there are pinion and juniper and acres of dry grass. We patrolled the area for a couple of hours, never seeing even a wisp of smoke. It was decided to head back into the Chaparral neighborhood and recheck that area.

We were in front of the firehouse, on our way to Chaparral Road, when a crew in Timberland Acres began calling for a water tender. I was not sure what they were doing, but it sounded as though they were requesting a tender at their location immediately. I heard Chief Price trying to contact Tender 3 on the radio. She told me to break away from Engine 3 and head out to T/A. I made a u-turn on the highway, flipped on the overhead emergency lights, hit the siren and made a beeline for Timberland Road. Winding my way back into the neighborhood, I got on the radio to request an exact location. Tim Dickinson answered and told me to go past the substation and up the hill. I followed his directions, rounded a bend in the road and came up on Engine 2. It took me approximately seven minutes from the time I received the call, to get on scene. Tim waved me up to the engine. I stopped the tender, threw on the airbrake and jumped out. I grabbed a "stinger hose" from a compartment on Tender 3 and hooked it up to the engine. After turning on the PTO switch and idling up the motor, I filled the engines' tank with water.

I could finally see why they needed the tender so quickly. There was a log sided shed, fully engulfed in flame, and it was only ten feet from a similarly constructed house. The house had been spared from the fire's initial run, but was now being threatened by this flaming shed. There was an engine from Payson on scene, as well as Engine 2, but they were both dangerously low on water. Once they had a good water supply, the fire was knocked down rather quickly. Before leaving the scene, I made sure that both of the fire trucks water tanks had been topped off. I stopped at the sub-station and filled up the tender, using the downspout.

I drove back to the Linden Fire main station. The situation was finally starting to quiet down here. We were starting to hear some numbers for containment of this fire. They were small, to be sure, but there was at least some good news. The fire was ten percent contained, meaning that a line had been cut around a portion of it. There were noticeably fewer firefighters at the station and the ones that *were* here were mostly local. Even though operations were winding down, I knew that the totality of this disaster had not yet sunk in. It was as if we were trying to control the bleeding on an injured patient without having done a complete assessment. First things first.

Walking into the station, I could see that the crew from the attack truck was getting ready to go out on patrol. They were going into Cheney Ranch to scour out any remaining hot spots, so I decided to follow along in the tender. I knew that some homes had been destroyed in there. I knew, also, that a couple of these homes were on Dreamy Draw, which is where the two Akitas had been penned. The homes were situated in the back of the subdivision and butted right up to the forest. Though it was mostly juniper and pinion, it was dense, and the fire had burned through the vegetation with an extreme fury. As we turned onto Dreamy Draw my stomach began to tighten in anticipation of what I would see.

We parked the vehicles and got out. The house where the two dogs had been was gone. The area was now unrecognizable from when Tim and I had fed and watered the Akitas. I saw that the chain-link pen, though badly warped, was still standing but the dog house was gone. Timidly, I stepped up and peered into the pen, expecting to see the burned carcasses of the dogs, but they were gone.

"What are you looking at?" one of the firefighters asked me.

"Oh, there were two dogs in here a couple of days ago," I replied. "Maybe somebody cut them loose before the fire came in here."

"Are you talking about those Akitas?" he asked. "They were taken to the shelter in Springerville."

What a relief! I could handle seeing the destruction caused by the fire and I knew that there would be plenty of human misery as well, but the toll that this was taking on the animals was difficult for me to deal with. Most people, myself included, made the choice to build a home in the forest. We would have to live with the consequences of our decision. The animals, however, had no such choice and were here because they were brought here by us or because this was their natural habitat. That the dogs had survived was one more bit of good news. We left Cheney Ranch and went back to the Linden Fire Department for lunch.

Chapter 26

Though there was still a good deal of smoke visible in Linden, the main body of the fire was now east of us. After lunch, I sat on the hood of the attack truck and watched two helicopters dropping buckets of water on a house that was south of the department. The home had been built high on a hill and the fire was at the base, trying to make a run upwards. The choppers were near surgical in the way they were pinpointing their drops and it looked as though they'd be able to save this structure.

Because of the location of the fire (it was starting to get dangerously close to Show Low now) there were several fire crews working to cut a line in the forest near Joe Tank Road. Tim Heim approached me and asked if I would take Tender 3 out to this area for a couple of hours. "They want a tender back there to soak the sides of the road. It's still pretty hot, and they're afraid the fire might run up to the road," he said.

"Sure, I'll do it," I replied. "How will I know who to talk to?"

Tim responded, "The IC is wearing a white hard hat. Just look for him. He'll tell you where they need you."

I jumped into Tender3, started it up and pulled out onto Highway 260. I could see a couple of brush trucks parked at the entrance to Joe Tank Road. I turned the tender onto the narrow, bumpy dirt road and drove back into the forest. After going about three-quarters of mile, I came across a clearing that had several trucks parked around it. I started looking for the IC in the white hat, but to my dismay, nearly everyone back here was wearing a white hard hat. It appeared as though everyone was breaking for lunch. Some of the crews were leaning against their trucks eating sandwiches, while others were stretched out on the ground, napping. Again, all the firefighters were wearing the yellow shirts and green pants, and I was still wearing the fluorescent orange jumpsuit. I stuck out like a sore thumb as I walked among them, trying to locate the person in charge.

Nobody seemed to know who or where the IC was. I was directed to a truck in the back of the clearing but I could not find anyone there who had requested this water tender. I started back to Tender 3. I would call Tim on the radio to find out what he wanted me to do, but before I reached my truck, I noticed two Fort Apache Hot Shot crews hastily putting away their lunch boxes, all of them looking off to the southwestern horizon. They were the only ones moving. The rest of the crews were still napping or eating their lunch. I quickened my pace towards the truck. The Hot Shots were packing up for a reason and I was going to follow their lead.

I jogged to the tender, opened the door and jumped in. It was going to be somewhat difficult to turn this big truck around on the narrow road. I would have to pull forward and back up several times before the nose of the truck was pointed in the direction of the highway. As I maneuvered the tender on the road, I looked in my rear-view mirror to see a huge plume of rolling, black smoke in the canyon below this meadow. By the time I got turned around, the Apache crews were several hundred yards ahead of me. I hit the gas and headed out to Highway 260.

When I reached the blacktop, the Apaches' trucks were parked off to the side of the road. I pulled the tender another hundred yards past them and got on the radio.

"Incident Command, this is Tender3," I said.

"Go ahead Tender 3." It was Tim. I explained to him that I was unable to locate a supervisor and that the hot shots had peeled out and that I was seeing a helluva lot of smoke back here. Did he know what was going on?

"It looks like the fire is getting legs again," he replied, "Just stay where you are until we get some better information." I didn't tell him that there was no way I was going back in there. The smoke was starting to get thick and black and the rest of the crews were starting to come out of the area. I opened the driver side door and watched the smoke column rise into the sky. "So, here we go," I thought to myself. "The push into Show Low is on."

I watched as truck after truck came off of Joe Tank Road and lined up on Highway 260. It was obviously too dangerous to be in there and I was glad I wasn't back on the dirt road trying to wet it down. That could have been a big mistake. The trees in there are tall and close together and it's possible that I wouldn't have seen the fire approaching until it was too late. In the space of twenty minutes the fire has exploded into an inferno. This is the moment the Forest Service and the city of Show Low have been dreading. The fire has roared back to life and it is knocking on the door.

I pulled the truck forward to try and get a better view into the area where the fire was most active. The smoke, however, was too dense to allow a glimpse into the canyon. I sat and watched as the fire grew, knowing that the next few hours would spell out the fate of thousands of people. If the fire were not stopped, it would run through the nearby neighborhoods and straight through downtown Show Low. Will this ever end? For a while, it had seemed that we had gained the upper hand on this monster, but as it has done so many times before, it has proven us to be wrong.

I caught a glimpse of something overhead and saw the great Sekorski helicopter flying into the plume of smoke. It had been drawing up water from Fool Hollow Lake, which is just a mile or so away, and was dropping its load on the head of the fire. As it flew off for another load of water, a gigantic double-rotor chopper replaced it. I assumed that it also was capable of dropping water. I had not seen this particular craft before. There were the smaller helicopters, with the bucket dangling from a line beneath them, but this one had been absent from the firefight. "*Now* we start the aerial assault," I thought. "What in the world took so long?"

The aircraft began hitting the fire with a vengeance heretofore unseen from the beginning of this disaster. I wondered why the fire had not been attacked in this manner when it was still in its infancy. If it were fought like this when it was still in Cibecue, it may not have reached Pinedale, or Clay Springs or Linden. Now that it is threatening Show Low, the big guns are being brought out in full force.

I radioed in to the station and asked if they wanted me to return to quarters or stay here on the top of Joe Tank Hill. I was told to wait here, just in case they were able to knock this fire down. I would be available to supply the crews with water, should they need it. After waiting another hour, it became obvious to me that this was, solely, an aerial show. They would not be using ground crews for quite a while because the fire was, simply, too hot. I called in to the station again and, this time was told to return. I started the tender and drove the mile and a half back to the Linden Fire Department.

I backed the tender into the parking lot and walked into the meeting room. There were several people standing in the parking lot, watching the various aircraft make their passes over the fire, but I had seen enough. When I found Tim Heim, I told him what I had seen while waiting at the top of Joe Tank Hill. He agreed with me that our resources would be better left in Linden now. Most of the Show Low Department had been pulled off of the fire several days ago in anticipation of it making its run into town. It was my understanding that they had been triaging the neighborhoods closest to where the fire would make its approach, so they would have most of their equipment poised to attack the flames, if and when they blew into town. Between Show Low's equipment, the Forest Service and Hot Shot crews and the many aircraft, it was doubtful that Linden Fire would be called upon to help out.

That was fine with me. We would be there in an instant if we were called, but I was getting burned out. I felt as though this would be our world from now on. Fighting a blaze that would continuously raise its head, no matter what we did to try and stop it. We would be trapped in a perpetual realm of fire. We would be trapped in Hell. Logically, I knew that the Rodeo-Chediski Fire would eventually come to an end, but after so many days of smoke, fire and destruction, I was not thinking in a logical fashion. I could tell by the haggard look on the faces of my friends and fellow firefighters that this fire was beginning to drain them also.

Yes, there are many resources from all over the country here to help out, but they will eventually go home to whatever state in which they live. This *is* where we live. Now that the fire has swept through here and is moving away, thoughts of recovery are lurking in the backs of our minds. It is too daunting to think about though. There will be an eternity to pore over the remnants of this disaster, but right now, we just want it to be over with.

Chapter 27

I was starting to feel depressed again and I'd found that moving around would help relieve a darkened mood. For a while. Stepping out into the parking lot, I saw a green and white SUV parked directly in front of the station. It was a Forest Service Law Enforcement vehicle, and there were two wet, black noses poking out of the rear window. I walked over and looked inside. Two beautiful black Labrador Retrievers began wagging their tails and slobbering all over my hand as I petted them. "Where did you guys come from?" I asked. Upon hearing my voice, they started to get even more animated, raising their paws up to the window, both vying for some attention. I reached in and scratched them behind the ears. This must have been to their liking because they quit moving around and leaned their heads into my hand as I scratched. "Are you guys thirsty? Want some water?" I asked. They wagged their tails intensely, so I went into the station to find a pan in which to put some water.

The woman who was driving the SUV was talking to some firefighters in the meeting room and I approached her and inquired about the dogs. Wearing a USFS Law Enforcement uniform, replete with side arm and badge, she too, looked tired. She told me that she had found the dogs running in a field near Highway 260 and Burton Road. Because they had no tags, they were to be taken to the shelter in Springerville until the fire was over. The people manning the shelter would try to reunite the dogs with their owner when things calmed down. The dogs wore only collars, with no ID or serial numbers, so this could prove to be difficult.

I found a metal pan, filled it to the top with water and took it out to the big, floppy dogs in the truck. They were very thirsty and lapped up nearly all of the water in a short time. Raising their heads, water dripping from their muzzles, they looked at me as if to say, "More please." I went back inside and refilled the pan. After the dogs had drunk their fill of water, I set the pan down and went into the bay where the dog chow was being stored. There was very little food left, most of it having already been distributed, but I found a can of cat food and decided to see if they would eat it. The two dogs wolfed it down in no time flat and I wished that I had something else to feed them. I knew that they would be headed for the shelter, which is over fifty miles away, and decided that they shouldn't make the ride on a full stomach. They would be well cared for there.

I wondered to myself, just how many pets had been displaced by this fire. The number of people who had been relocated was vast. I'm sure that not all of them had pets and the one's that did, surely would have taken them along, but I have already seen many animals that were left behind to fend for themselves. Some people have a mistaken notion that animals will simply run away from fire, or that their "wild" instincts will take over and they will be able to survive on their own. This is not true. Horses have been known to run back into burning stalls, thinking that they would be safe there, and I've seen enough starving dogs on the Reservation to know that they do not revert to a wild animal capable of killing enough prey to feed themselves. If this catastrophic event is hard on humans, then it is doubly hard on the animals that we have taken into our care. My thoughts turned to Carol and our own cats. How were they handling the stress of being in an unknown environment? Hopefully, I will be able to get them home soon.

It was looking as though Linden was now in the clear from the fire. It was continuing to threaten Show Low but, so far, had not made a direct attack on the city. The prevailing wind direction was pushing the fire to our east and it was highly unlikely that it would be able to burn back into our area. I thought that it might be safe to bring Carol and our cats back home at this point and decided to talk to Chief Price about doing just that. I had learned from Dewayne that his wife, Pam, had driven in from Prescott and was with Carol at the house in White Mountain Lake. I asked if he thought it would be wrong to smuggle them back in to Linden, even though the rest of the community had not been cleared to return. Dewayne and I were both of the same mindset. The fire would not come back into Linden and, other than the residual smoke, there would be no danger in bringing the girls home.

I began to formulate a plan. I would need two Linden Fire Department shirts, one for Carol and one for Pam, and the rescue truck. I should be able to get them through the roadblock at Lone Pine Dam Road and Highway 77 if they looked as though they were members of the department. I went back into the meeting room and went upstairs to talk to the chief. Marilyn was on the phone when I walked into her office. I sat down and waited for her to finish her conversation and then brought up the idea of bringing Carol and Pam back home. Though she would not give me her explicit approval, I could tell that she thought that the danger of the fire making a return visit to Linden was remote. She told me that if I did bring them back, the girls would have to lay low and not venture out into the Linden area. The Sheriff's Office was still on the lookout for looters and burglars and there could be a problem if they were seen.

I knew that both Pam and Carol would stay put. Carol had been gone from home for well over a week now and I knew that she glad to be able sleep in her own bed and have the cats in an environment that was familiar to them.

I called Carol on my cell phone and told her about the clandestine plan that I was hatching. She was ecstatic upon hearing about it, and wanted to come home immediately. I told her that it would be better if we waited until morning. She would have time to pack and get the cats ready and I would be able to round up the shirts, and even hats, if I could find them. After much discussion, she reluctantly agreed and, before I hung up, I told her that I would be there bright and early in the morning. I was able to get two shirts and one hat from Carol Lewis, who had some spare shirts in a cupboard in her office. After inviting anyone who wanted a place to sleep to my house, I went home for the evening.

Tonight, there would be Tim Heim, Ryan Turner, Garry Moore and myself at the house. I told them that after tonight they would have to sleep elsewhere, because I wanted to have the next few evenings alone, with Carol. After a couple of cocktails, I turned in for the evening and barely slept a wink.

I arose before sunrise, knowing that Carol had probably not slept well last night either. We were both just as excited as children on Christmas Eve. I made a pot of coffee and after it was brewed, poured myself a cup and stepped out onto the front porch. I was alarmed at the amount of smoke in the air. It was so dense that I couldn't see across the front yard and I began to worry that perhaps the fire had somehow changed direction during the night. As the day grew brighter, however, the smoke began to lift and the morning sky seemed brighter than previous days. I went inside and hastily cooked breakfast for everyone and then drove to the station.

Chapter 28

It was almost 8:00 a.m. when I pulled away from the station in Rescue. Although I had taken a quick shower this morning, I kept looking in the mirror. I felt like a teenager on his first date. The orange coveralls were dirty and covered in soot and ash, but I wore them anyway so as not to arouse suspicion when I went through the roadblock. I drove out onto Highway 260 and made a left onto Lone Pine Dam Road.

There was a faint haze in the air but the morning was beautiful. Even though it was nearly July, the mountain air had a crisp coolness to it. I looked towards Show Low and saw that the smoke was not billowing up the way it had done yesterday. It appeared that it had moved slightly south, which would put it behind Show Low and not at its front door step. For the first time since this fire had begun, I felt a sense of hope. No. It was more than that. I could feel in my bones that this ordeal would soon be over. I knew it with certainty. It was a wondrous feeling.

I drove slowly down Lone Pine Dam Road. I wanted to savor the morning. The sun, though fairly high in the sky, had an orange blush to it, making it seem as though the morning hours would last all day.

This road has changed a great deal since Carol and I first moved to the mountain. The trees along here use to be a thick mix of juniper and pinion. I remember stopping along the roadside to search for the delectable nuts from the pinion tree, most of the trees being loaded with the delicate, paper-thin cones. Back then, the trees were all a deep, rich, green color. Then a change began to occur. It was almost imperceptible at first. A few trees, usually spaced closely together, would turn brown and die. The next year, more and more of them died off and now, five years later, there is hardly a pinion left on Lone Pine Dam Road. This scene has played out in many locations in northern Arizona. The bark beetle is the culprit and it has decimated the pinion pine population, in some areas reaching 100% mortality.

This morning, however, I overlook the demise of the pinion and relish driving through a forested area that is not smoldering.

The roadblock was in place and I waved as I drove through. The police were not so much interested in the people leaving as they were in the people returning to the evacuated areas and I knew that we would be looked at more closely when we returned. I turned right on White Mountain Lake Road and drove to the house where Carol and Pam were waiting. I could tell that the girls were excited to be going home. Carol had some of her belongings packed and sitting outside the house when I pulled up. I gave Carol and Pam their Linden Fire shirts and they went inside to change. We packed as much of their stuff as could fit, into the cab of the truck and, after loading up the cats, began the return trip to Linden.

The much-anticipated roadblock turned out to be somewhat anticlimactic. I stopped the rescue truck and the officer asked where I was going. I told him that we were returning to Linden and we were waved through. With the anxiety of passing through the roadblock behind us, the mood in the truck became much lighter. We began to joke and laugh. I told the girls, in a mock accent, that I would be able to get a high price for them on the fire line. "All the women out there smell like smoke, but you girls smell nice and clean!" Pam and Carol laughed and called me their "coyote," a south of the border term for smuggler. I liked the nickname and I drove on, feeling daring and dangerous.

As we got closer to Linden, I could still see smoke rising up on the horizon. The fire was slowly being brought under control, but there were still some very hot areas behind Show Low. I told both of the women that they would have to keep a low profile once we were home, per Marilyn, and that they should not answer the door if someone knocked. When I pulled into our driveway, it was all I could do to keep the cats from jumping out. They too would have to stay inside for a few days, but it would be much easier on them, being in familiar territory.

We unloaded Carol's things first and then drove across the road to Dewayne's and unloaded Pam's items. Before returning the rescue truck to the station, I went inside our house to help Carol unpack. She was giddy at the thought of being home and, even though I still had our clothes and pictures in my truck at the station, she remarked that our house looked perfect. I understood her sentiments because I would have the very same thought every time I had been able to return. I told Carol that I had to get back to the station. Before I left, I hugged her and told her, "I'm glad to have you back. Welcome home, Honey."

I took the rescue truck back to the station and parked it. The Linden Fire Department, once a beehive of activity, was unusually quiet. As the fire was winding down, the many resources that had been available to us were either being sent out of the state to other wildfires or, were being sent to Show Low to guard against any run the fire may try to make there. With the exception of the wisps of smoke that were still rising from the hillsides, Linden was slowly returning to the peaceful valley to which I was accustomed. The evacuation was still in effect and that added to the eerie serenity. There were no barking dogs, no clamor from semi-trucks rumbling down the highway and not a sound from the nearby construction yard. Also noticeably absent was the drone of helicopters. This had been the background music for the fire. Whether they were firefighting choppers, news choppers, police choppers or military choppers, the thumping rotor blades were a ubiquitous sound that seemed to accompany us wherever we were located during the fire.

I walked back to the cinder pit to get my truck. There were still a few personal vehicles parked here, but the fire trucks and tenders had been relocated to the main station. I started my truck and drove home to unload the cabinets full of tapes, clothing, photos and other items I had retrieved when it appeared that our house would be doomed. This would be another step in returning our home to "normal."

Carol helped me bring everything back inside and, after putting our stuff away, suggested that we soak in our hot tub for a while. The idea of lounging in the tub seemed almost alien to me. I agreed, but after two weeks of hectic activity that had been punctuated by moments of sheer terror, the thought of simply sitting and relaxing just seemed out of place. When I slid down into the hot water I felt the many days of walking through the ashes slowly ebbing away.

Our neighborhood was silent except for the call of a bird that I could not identify. It was a high-pitched "caw" that reached a crescendo and then tapered off to silence. It sounded like an exotic species, something not native to the mountain. I knew that there was a ranch approximately a mile away where they raised peacocks and I assumed that one of them had escaped during the initial evacuation. The lonely call of the bird seemed to symbolize the sentiment I was feeling. I knew that we had tried to do our best while fighting the fire, and I knew that the fire was winding down, but there was a palpable sense of loss that permeated the air. Something was gone and it would never be replaced. The joy of having Carol and our cats back home was tempered by a feeling of melancholy for the people who had lost their homes and for the loss of our once beautiful forest. I closed my eyes and tried to let all of my emotions melt away into the hot water.

Chapter 29

Over the next few days the containment numbers on the fire started going up. At first 10%, then 20% and finally 90% contained. To call the fire fully contained would not be accurate. The fire, we were told, would probably burn underground or smolder in the numerous snags until the snow started to fall. When the residents of the mountain were allowed to return home, we would probably be chasing smoke and flare-ups for a long time. We expected this. When the evacuation was declared over, about June 29th, we braced for what we knew would be a very busy few weeks.

Life at my house seemed to have slowed to a crawl. There was no hurry to do anything. Little situations that would have been irritating in the past were now shrugged off with the knowledge that we had been spared the fate of many of our friends and neighbors. Put into perspective were the things that truly mattered most. Things like love, trust and friendship.

Nozzle and his family had begun staying with Carol and me. We were delighted to be able to help them in such a small way until they were able to figure out what they would be doing. They, like so many others, had the daunting task of running through the bureaucratic maze of insurance companies and federal assistance programs to help get them back on their feet.

Nozzle had been having doubts about whether he should rebuild on the same property. He and I drove out to Timberland Acres, where his house once stood, and looked over the area. Though his home was mere rubble, the larger picture was more encouraging. His home had been framed with huge, old oak trees and, though they were singed, I thought that they would survive. He had lost a couple of big pine trees and the hillside behind his home had been scorched. As we stood in what was once his driveway, we tried to imagine what this area would look like in a couple of years.

Across the road, the forest had been untouched by the fire, so he would still have a tree-lined view from his front window. The sides of his home would also have a few trees close by. "I would have no problem rebuilding here Noz," I told him. "These oak will come back and you still have green in a lot of places. You're going to have a good deal of clean up work to do, but once that's done, your lot should look pretty good." I could tell that he was wrestling with the idea. It had to seem like an insurmountable task to return his property to its former state, but I would do all I could to convince him that, even though his home had burned, his land was in relatively good condition. I think that, after seeing what the fire has wrought in other areas of T/A, he will realize that he is indeed fortunate to have a few trees still alive.

Other residents of Timberland Acres had fared far worse than Nozzle. Many people were brought back into T/A by bus to see their homes and property in its post-fire state. Having seen first hand the devastation the fire brought to this neighborhood, I cannot imagine what the bus ride was like. Even though I had been through Timberland Acres several times, the scene always seemed uglier with each visit. The amount of work that it will take to get this area back to a livable condition is unfathomable. I would think that it must have been a solemn ride, punctuated with tears and disbelief, as they viewed the remains of a neighborhood scarred beyond recognition.

As suspected, when the residents of Linden returned, we began to get a number of calls. Most were due to smoke from trees that were still smoldering. Because of the long drought, there was simply no moisture in the ground, and the root systems of the juniper and manzanita became a network of underground embers. We would respond when called and soak whatever hot spots the homeowners found and move on to the next one. One thing that I had not planned on was what I had termed "gray ghosts." The warm, daytime air would mix with the cooler air leftover from the night and form whirlwinds. These "dust devils" would run through the ash, which covered the ground like powder, and send it high into the air. From a distance it looked exactly like a column of smoke. We would be chasing these phantoms for months until rain or snow soaked the ash and kept it plastered to the ground.

There were some instances when a call to the fire department was necessary. Several times we got on scene to find a snag of trees or a stump that was hot enough to erupt into flame. This scenario would usually occur in an area that had burned exceedingly hot and, though the chance for it spreading was slim, we would soak the surrounding area and turn the soil with shovels to extinguish every ember.

Chasing down erupting flame and hot spots would be the norm for the next few weeks. As the folks in Linden and the other communities ravaged by fire came home, they would find the fire hidden in some nook on their property and someone from the fire department would come and extinguish it.

A week after the fire broke out, President George W. Bush made a visit to the gymnasium in Springerville. This had been home to a number of the evacuees during the fire. After praising the people there for their endurance and fortitude, he declared the mountain a disaster area. By doing so, it allowed a great deal of federal money to start flowing into the region.

His appearance was a huge emotional boost to the people in the gym and was a display of responsible leadership, in my opinion. I can't speak for the other firefighters who were battling this fire, but when I heard that the President was in Springerville, it brought home the immensity of the situation. I felt as though we were being supported in our effort and had a shoulder to lean on if we needed it. The federal money released to the area would allow the small rural departments to upgrade their equipment and would help put many people to work trying to rebuild the incinerated neighborhoods.

I was thankful, every time I drove home, that I still had trees and more importantly, a house to return to. The bulk of the Linden valley had been spared the wrath of the fire. The drive along Highway 260 is unmarred until you reach the foothills of Timberland Acres. It is only window dressing. The forest that lies on the other side of the ridge is decimated. In all, nearly 500,000 acres of forest is gone. Up in smoke. The toll on the wildlife is unknown. The toll on the people of this area is very visible and the fire will continue to haunt us for years, I'm afraid. These mountain people are a resilient bunch though, and I am reminded of the words of the firefighters from Kentucky on the night the fire burned into Linden. "Ain't no little fire gonna keep us from eatin' supper." The communities on this mountain will survive.

Chapter 30

The fire would be declared fully contained on July 8th. The days from June 18th to July 8th would be the longest in my life, to this point. As things calmed down in Linden, most of us would get back to our day-to-day routines. Our bi-monthly training had been put on hiatus for a while. The firefighters on the Linden Fire Department had been through a true baptismal by fire and the thought of training so soon after the battle we'd been through seemed redundant.

Three weeks after containment of the fire, we were called in to a special training. I had no idea what we would be doing, but I was anxious to see how the other firefighters had been coping. We had pretty much been tending to our own home life and had not seen much of each other, with the exception of when we had been called out on a smoke chase.

I walked into the meeting room to see nearly all of the Linden Fire Department in attendance. One person who I thought would be absent was Bob Filley. Word had it that, after he learned of the destruction of his home, he flew to some Caribbean island to be surrounded by water. Actually, he had gone to Phoenix for a couple of days, but he had returned and was here at the meeting.

The conversation among the firefighters was varied and pertained mostly to what we had seen and done during the fire. Chief Price went to the front of the room and explained that there were some people who wanted to speak to the Linden Fire Department this evening. A few minutes later, two gentlemen walked into the meeting room. It was Larry Humphrey and Roy Hall. They were the Incident Commander and Operations Commander on this fire, respectively.

Humphrey walked to the front of the room and promptly turned his back to the people seated in front of him. I watched as he took a tin of chewing tobacco from his back pocket and loaded a wad in his cheek. He turned back around and looked at us with a gleam in his eye, one cheek bulging from the tobacco. He proceeded to tell us what a fine job we had done and how we were invaluable to the firefighting effort and the mission could not have been accomplished without us. Roy Hall stepped up to the front of the room and, basically, parroted what Humphrey had been saying. He told us that he had grown up in Vernon, a little town outside of Show Low, and understood the needs of the rural communities. There were a couple of firefighters in the room that had also been raised in Vernon, but they could not remember Roy Hall ever living there.

After fifteen minutes of heaping praise upon us, he opened the meeting to questions. We had a bunch of them. Why had the fire not been attacked immediately when it was in Cibecue? Why were resources pulled out of areas ahead of the fire? Why, when the fire was in Pinedale, were all firefighters and equipment ordered to go to Show Low? Why hadn't the air tankers been sent up early in the day to attack the fire, instead of waiting until the crack of noon? Why was the fire attacked full-force when it threatened Show Low, but allowed to burn through the smaller, rural communities? The look in their eyes told us that they couldn't believe what they were hearing. This ragtag group of firefighters were questioning their judgment and they didn't like it one bit.

Tim Heim, who worked for the Forest Service, had drawn up some maps of the Timberland Acres neighborhood showing where the fire hydrants and stock ponds were located. He had passed the maps out to Forest Service people in T/A before the fire ran through the area. When he asked Roy Hall why they hadn't been used, Hall responded, "How long have you worked for the Forest Service?" Tim replied that he had been there a few months. "So, that makes you an expert, huh?" Hall asked.

His response did not go over well with the Linden Fire Department personnel. We had busted our rumps trying to fight this fire and it seemed that the Forest Service from the beginning had hampered our efforts. Many in the group began to loudly voice their objections to Roy Hall's verbal assault on Tim. Like the rest of us, Tim had been trying to help the Forest Service. We knew the region. These two guys had never been here before.

I looked to the back of the room and saw Larry Humphrey lifting his middle finger on one hand and pointing towards the door with the other hand, as if to say, "Screw these guys. Let's go." Several other firefighters saw his gesture and decided to leave. I stood up and headed for the door.

These two guys came in here patting themselves on the back, expecting us to be in awe of them. When we began asking hard questions regarding the manner in which they fought the fire, they became indignant, refusing to answer our questions and verbally attacking one of our own firefighters. If this meeting was supposed to assuage our anger at the Forest Service for letting the fire run unabated through our communities, it failed miserably. I went out to my truck and drove home.

In my view, this meeting had pretty well summed up the feelings between the rural fire departments and the Forest Service. The firefighters from Heber-Overgaard, Pinedale-Clay Springs and Linden felt that the fire should have been attacked before it made its push into our communities. Had it been hit hard while it was still on the Reservation, it was possible that it would have never made it up the Rim and into our towns and neighborhoods. These local departments also thought that civilian resources should have been utilized in the suppression of the fire. Many of the ranchers and farmers have their own heavy equipment that could (and should) have been used to cut firebreaks outside of the towns that were hit so hard. We also wondered why the Rim Road had not been utilized more efficiently.

When first built, the Rim Road was supposed to be a firebreak that would help prevent any fire, that started below the Rim, from running up to the top. We felt that this road should have been widened with bulldozers while the fire was still on the Reservation and below the Rim. The Forest Service, on the other hand, took a "wait and see" stance that allowed the fire to gain strength and go out of control. They considered any civilian resources to be a liability and, therefore, did not regard them as being of any value. Why the Forest Service never utilized the Rim Road is a mystery. Why the fire was allowed to burn on the day it was started is still in dispute.

One story that I have heard concludes that the fire was encroaching on sacred land on the Apache Reservation. The area held burial sites and many artifacts and an anthropologist was called in to survey the region before the dozers could start cutting a line in front of the fire. The anthropologist either didn't arrive, or arrived too late, and the fire started to run out of control. By this time it was impossible to keep the fire where it was and it exploded the next day. Once it became obvious that the fire would run up onto the Rim, the Forest Service backed off, saying that it was just too dangerous to try and stop the fire when it was in the pines. They would let the fire burn until it ran into the smaller scrub and grass and then it would be attacked.

If you look at the larger picture, you see that Heber-Overgaard was hit broadside by the fire. There were no firebreaks cut by the Forest Service and they did not allow the civilian crews, which had been assembled and ready to work, to cut any fire line. The fire ran unabated into Pinedale and Clay Springs. When the fire got into town, every piece of firefighting equipment was pulled out, on the orders of the Forest Service, and sent to a field five miles away. When a crew from Clay Springs (and eventually Linden) broke ranks from the Forest Service to try and defend their homes, they were branded as renegades. The fire burned into Timberland Acres and Linden, and the bulk of the equipment was sent to Show Low. The local fire department was sent out of T/A when it was discovered that they were cutting their own firebreak. It was not until the fire reared up close to Show Low that a major aerial assault was launched. Show Low escaped the wrath of the fire, losing only an acre or two.

The hand signals that Larry Humphrey gave to Roy Hall during the meeting at the Linden Fire Department said it all.

Screw these guys.

Let's go.

Chapter 31

The Rodeo-Chediski Fire is now an event of the past for most Arizonans. Unless you live in one of the communities that were burned, the only time you think of it is when you make the drive from Payson to Show Low. The thousands of dead trees bear silent testimony to the inferno that swept over this area two years ago. Many of these trees are beginning to decay and will likely be blown to the ground when the spring wind starts to blow.

If you are a skier, and we have received snow, you likely will notice the huge white swaths on the mountain where the trees no longer have leaves or needles to hide the snow. The burned areas appear to be highlighted. Shortly after the fire was out, an Apache woman told me that snow would heal the land. I hope she is right, because there is much healing that needs to be done.

The long-term consequences of the fire and the drought are unknown. I wonder, for instance, how the bark beetle infestation will affect the wildlife in this region? The beetles have decimated the drought-weakened pinion trees. The nuts that they produce have been in the food chain for hundreds, if not thousands of years. Now that the pinion nut has been removed from the equation, I wonder if there will be a rippling effect on the other animals that live in the forest?

The effects of drought are many-facetted and not only encompass the devastation of the pinion, but figure into the wildfire season as well. Fires have been hotter, faster and more destructive than in the past. The way I see it is that we have reached a moment in time where many things have come together that will change the forest, as we know it, forever. By combining the total fire-suppression of the last hundred years, the lack of moisture caused by the lingering drought, the bark beetle infestation and the wildland urban-interface situation, our forests are ripe for another similarly catastrophic wildfire. Should the drought end today, I don't know that the pine forest would be able to recover.

Our great-grandchildren will walk through a different forest. My guess is that it will be a hardwood forest as opposed to the great coniferous forest that we have grown accustomed to. If the U.S.D.A. Forest Service had *not* implemented the idea that all forest fires were bad and needed to be extinguished immediately, would that have been enough to save the forest? I don't know. A forest needs rain to flourish and we are stuck in a drought cycle that some climatologic "experts" predict could linger on for decades. Insects have always been a natural part of the environment, but with an outbreak of bark beetles that borders on epic proportions, can the forest survive? Again, I don't know.

My sense is that Mother Nature knows what she is doing. It is possible that what we are witnessing is a natural reaction to a natural situation. The deserts and forests have never remained static. There has always been change. One only has to visit the Petrified Forest in northern Arizona to see that this is true. Millions of years ago, there was a mighty coniferous forest in this region, which is now mostly sand and sagebrush.

The human toll that the Rodeo-Chediski fire has exacted is harder to figure. The homes that were burned can, for the most part, be rebuilt. Trees can be replanted. The way of life before the fire, however, no longer exists. Where once, the forest was a friendly, hospitable place to live, we have learned that it can also be deadly. We thought that we would

Gary Phillip Holdcroft

be able to manage the forest and learned, to a certain degree, that the forest must manage itself.

There are certain things that we, as forest-dwellers, can do to improve our ability to live in balance with the natural surroundings. We can thin the trees from our property and we can deep water our favorite trees to enable them to get through the drought, but we can never go back to the idyllic notion that the forest is our Eden. There is a responsibility that goes with living in the trees and grasslands that must be adhered to.

We cannot set fire to the forest in order to gain employment. We cannot put a wall around the forest and not let people in to enjoy it, as some environmentalists think we should do. Should we choose to live in the forest, we must assume the consequences of our actions. If a fire runs over your house, it will burn. If the drought continues on for years, the likelihood of your house burning increases. These are simple notions but they seem to have been ignored by the ever-increasing population of people living in the communities that are surrounded by trees. The Rodeo-Chediski Fire has proven to me that forces greater than ourselves will dictate how we live in the woods.

Chapter 32

It would take a full year for me to revisit some of the areas where I fought the fire. I have been through Timberland Acres many times, even going so far as buying a chainsaw to help some of the residents remove the charred trees from their properties. But for some reason, I just did not want to see Pinedale or Clay Springs or Heber-Overgaard. I wanted to remember them in their former green state. I'd talked to people who had made the drive west on Highway 260 and heard their stories of the devastated towns and the huge swaths of forest that had been reduced to charcoal, but I did not want see it for myself.

I suppose there are those who would read some deep, psychological meaning into this. I have heard the term, post-traumatic stress, bandied about as pertaining to the firefighters that worked so hard on the fire, but in my case, I don't think this is accurate. It's more the feeling of someone who has been disfigured, not wanting to look in the mirror. I knew it would be bad but I wasn't ready to face it.

One afternoon, Dewayne asked if I wanted to ride along with him to Heber. There was a produce stand there that was selling tomatoes and plums and a host of other fruits and vegetables. I said yes, ignoring the twinge of fear inside, and hopped in his Jeep to get my first view of the communities that had been impacted by the fire.

As we crested Juniper Ridge, which was as far west as I had been, I took in my first view of the meadow that had served as a staging area when the fire burned into Pinedale. The tree line behind the meadow was badly burned, but the field itself looked just as it had when we were last there. Driving through Pinedale, I saw that the wooden bridge was still standing, as was the barn where the chestnut mare had been pacing about on the night that Bob Filley and I were here. Looking closer, I could see a horse prancing around in the corral. The mare had survived!

The immediate entrance to Pinedale was relatively unchanged, but the hills to the south were scorched. Where there had once been green, there was now a dark-brown hue. Many of the pines in town, however, were unscathed.

The rest of the trip to Heber-Overgaard was made more palatable with the knowledge that the horse had survived the inferno in Pinedale. The Clay Springs area was similarly burned, with the hills to its south and west painted the same brown tint. This will be the color of the burned areas for many years to come. Some spots between Clay Springs and Heber were absolutely decimated by the fire, but as we made the journey westward I could feel a slight easing of the anxiety I had felt before we left. It was bad. There was no doubt about it. But in the midst of the blackened forest I could see patches of bright green where young oak trees were sending up new shoots. There were areas of green grass, as well as the feathery leaves of the young, wild locust trees. The forest was awakening from its post-fire sleep.

As we entered Heber-Overgaard, I could see that Bison Ranch, the fabricated Old West town, was still standing. Again, the forest to the south was blackened, the trees looking like jagged sticks against the horizon. I was not quite prepared for the amount of damage I would see in Heber.

Whole neighborhoods in this town had succumbed to the fire. Yet, in the midst of the debris, there were signs of the townspeople rebuilding. Piles of burned lumber and charred trash had been piled up in front of the road and new homes were being built where the old ones had stood. While I had been afraid to come and witness the damage here, these people had looked it in the eye and were taking steps to recover from it. The timidity I was feeling had been overcome with a sense of pride in being part of the mountain community.

We found the farmers market at the west end of town, and after purchasing a sack of green chiles and a few fresh, sweet peaches, began the return trip to Linden. I was glad that Dewayne had invited me along for this drive. The devastation was worse than I had expected, but now I knew what our mountain looked like from Linden to Heber. There was one other thing I had to see, though. When we came back through Pinedale, I asked Dewayne to drive back to Danish Hollow Road.

He turned the Jeep onto the narrow blacktop leading into town. We passed the Pinedale Fire Station. It had burned to the ground and all that was left was the twisted metal roof of the Quonset hut. In the meadow behind the station, I could see the house that Bob and I had foamed was still standing. I remembered the flames coming over the top of Turkey Hill, and thought of the couple that were going to call this home. I was glad that it had survived. We drove out of town and headed towards Danish Hollow Road.

This area had been hit extremely hard. The ground looked like granite. There were very few signs of the forest making a comeback here. We took the doglegged road back to the house where Bob and I had stayed the night before the fire came through here. The house was gone.

Dewayne stopped the Jeep, and I stepped out to walk through the property. I looked to where the house once stood and all that was left was the rock walkway that had once lead to the front door. I felt as if I were standing in a graveyard. The wind whispered through the dead trees as I surveyed the ruins of what was once someone's home. There was blackened silverware scattered about where the kitchen had been. Unrecognizable pieces of metal lay in twisted heaps around the area and the scent of burnt wood still hung in the air.

I stood there in silence for a few minutes, listening to the wind blow through the bare branches of the trees.

"OK. I've seen enough," I told Dewayne, and we got back in the Jeep and started to drive away.

I turned and looked back toward the house. Something appeared to be moving several yards away. Off in the distance, I thought I saw an old, gray cat, running through the charcoal forest.

Epilogue

As I write, over two years have gone by since the Great Fire. There have been other big fires since then, but none on such a grand scale as the Rodeo-Chediski. Lightning sparked the Kinishba Fire of 2003. It burned close to 100,000 acres before a summer thunderstorm aided in putting it out. That same year, in my hometown of Tucson, the Aspen Fire obliterated thousands of acres of forest and decimated the picturesque village of Summerhaven. There have been fires on the Arizona-New Mexico border and, more recently, a huge fire near the town of Payson, Arizona. Lightning also set off this fire.

The Aspen Fire (84,750 acres and 335 structures burned) was a near carbon copy of what happened during the Rodeo-Chediski Fire. It was human caused and was not attacked until it began threatening the summer homes and businesses at the top of the mountain. Larry Humphreys' Type I team was assigned to *this* fire, as well as the Cerro Grande Fire in New Mexico (47,650 acres and 235 structures burned) and the Rodeo-Chediski conflagration (467,066 acres and 426 structures burned). All three fires consumed countless acres of coniferous forest and hundreds of homes and businesses. There would appear, to me, to be a pattern taking shape here.

I am not a professional firefighter. I volunteered with the Linden Fire Department, thinking it was a good way to serve the community in which I lived. Had I known when I joined the department that I would be involved in fighting the largest fire in Arizona's history, I may have had second thoughts. That being said, I would not trade the experience for anything. I learned a great deal about the people on this mountain and saw, firsthand, the gritty determination exhibited by the small, rural fire departments when they were faced with a crisis of immense proportion. I am proud of each and every one of them and am honored to call myself a volunteer firefighter.

I am not alone in questioning the judgment of the Forest Service. I am reminded of the meeting at the Linden Fire Department with Roy Hall and Larry Humphrey. When I asked Roy Hall if a more aggressive stance toward fighting the fire could have been taken, he responded, "Hey, nobody got hurt or killed and that is the thing that's most important." Well, OK, I agree. That *is* very important. The same result, however, could have been achieved if everybody had stayed home and not showed up to help fight the Rodeo-Chediski Fire. All the resources and equipment that were in place should have been used more aggressively. This is not only *my* opinion but that of many other people as well.

Had the "renegades" not taken a more forceful stance, there would have been more homes lost in Clay Springs. Had the Forest Service, the BIA, the Fire Management crews and all of the other governmental agencies in place in Cibecue taken a tougher stance, the fire may never have breached the Mogollon Rim. My hope is that some lessons have been learned.

As I said, I am not a professional firefighter. I can only speak to what I saw and heard while helping my department. Perhaps greater minds than mine can find a solution to some of the questions raised during the fires of the past few years. Hopefully, they will find some way to prevent the absolute destruction of our forests and communities.

The fire *has* changed our lives. Most of the people that were on the Linden Fire Department during the fire are still here. A few have quit and some have moved away. Some of our firefighters are now divorced. Tim Heim moved to Heber and still does seasonal work for the Forest Service. Larry Humphrey has since retired. Nozzle rebuilt his house on the same lot, but this time he has block skirting and a beautiful wooden deck that encompasses the entire home. Bob Filley also rebuilt on his own lot, as did Ed Dwyer. Thankfully, Chief Price never did get her Grecian tub. That old cowboy cook wouldn't part with his biscuit recipe, but I haven't given up hope. I may be able to track him down, yet!

Carol and I bought a small travel trailer so that, in the event of another evacuation, there will be a place to stay for her, the cats and our newest family member, our dog Mitzi. She was approximately five weeks old when I found her alongside the road in the small village of Cedar Creek.

The burned area *is* visible from all corners of Linden. The view from nearly everyone's home has changed. My home sits lower than most, so I only see the scars from the fire when I'm on the highway. I am more fortunate than many of my friends and neighbors because the trees around my house are still green. There are times when I will sit on our porch and simply gaze at them, wondering if I would have had the determination to rebuild if the fire had swept through here. I don't know. I *do* know that I cherish the view and feel sorry for those who no longer have one.

The fire is out now. This morning, however, the wind is blowing.

Again.

THE END

Gary Phillip Holdcroft